IF ONLY
YOU RECOGNIZED
GOD'S GIFT

If Only You Recognized God's Gift

John's Gospel as an Illustration of
Theological Reflection

Robert L. Kinast

WILLIAM B. EERDMANS PUBLISHING COMPANY
GRAND RAPIDS, MICHIGAN

3/3/99 9mr

Copyright © 1993 by Wm. B. Eerdmans Publishing Co.
255 Jefferson Ave. S.E., Grand Rapids, Michigan 49503

Printed in the United States of America

Library of Congress Cataloging-in-Publication Data

Kinast, Robert L.
If only you recognized God's gift: John's Gospel as an illustration of
theological reflection / Robert L. Kinast.
          p.   cm.
ISBN 0-8028-0673-2 (pbk.)
    1. Bible. N.T. John — Devotional use.   2. Bible. N.T. John — Theology.
I. Title.
BS2615.5.K56   1993
226.5'06 — dc20   92-40426
                                              CIP

*To my Scripture professors
who helped me recognize
God's gift in the Word*

*and to Judith,
who helps me recognize
God's gift in the world.*

Contents

Introduction   xi

1   **What Is Theological Reflection?**   1
    Clinical Pastoral Education   1
    Liberation Theology   2
    Theological Reflection   3
    John's Gospel   5

2   **The Goal of Theological Reflection**   9
    John the Baptizer   10
    The Baptizer's Disciples   13
    Royal Official   17
    Mary Magdalene   20
    The Disciples on the Sea   22
    Summary   25

3   **Obstacles to Theological Reflection**   27
    Reliance on External Authority   28

Cleansing of the Temple
Cure at Bethesda
Feast of Booths
Feast of Dedication

Lack of Imagination   43
Nicodemus
The Last Supper Discourse

Self-Protection   50
The Adulteress
Anointing at Bethany
Dialogue with Pilate

Summary   61

4   **Theological Reflection during a
    Ministerial Event**   63

Jesus and the Samaritan Woman   64
Setting
Entry
Theological Learning
Enactment

Summary   75

5   **Theological Reflection in a Group**   77

Cure of the Blind Man   78
Event
First Reactions
Experts
Personal Testimony
Confrontation
Recognition

Summary   89

6 **From Reflection to Praxis** 91

The Raising of Lazarus 92
Prelude
Theological Reflection
Praxis

Washing the Disciples' Feet 99

Cana 102

Summary 105

7 **The Action-Reflection Cycle** 107

Feeding of the Multitude 108

Summary 117

Epilogue 119

Introduction

A bout thirty-five years ago a revolution began in pastoral studies. It consisted in the simple proposition that the experience of ministering ought to teach the minister something about theology, not just about the skills for doing ministry. What it taught often turned out to be more realistic and insightful than a lot of the lessons learned in the classroom. Understandably this created tension (and sometimes conflict) on seminary faculties, a condition which still exists in some places.

The champions of this new pastoral theology (Seward Hiltner, Carroll Wise, Wayne Oates, Daniel Day Williams, Frank Lake) were not anti-intellectual; they valued scholarly theology and even contributed to it. But they also believed that the ministry had its own theological contribution to make. In this respect they were following an impulse as old as Christianity itself (and Judaism before that), for Christianity is not primarily a set of doctrines revealed from heaven but a set of experiences generated on earth.

Learning theology from experience (or "doing theological reflection") follows this impulse. It isn't easy. In fact, one of the preoccupations of pastoral studies in the last decade has been to develop models to do this very thing.

The present book is part of this effort. It goes back to the origins of Christianity, specifically to the Gospel of John. Rereading this Gospel with a theological reflector's eye is like reading a primer in the art so recently rediscovered. The purpose is to learn what John's Gospel can teach about theological reflection. There are pitfalls.

John's Gospel was not written for this purpose. It has its own integrity, which must be respected even while bringing a contemporary interest like theological reflection to the text. In itself this is valid. Believers do it all the time. But it must be done with care and respect for the results of scholarly exegesis.

John's authority cannot be extended to any conclusions about theological reflection. If useful patterns or guiding principles for modern theological reflection are discerned in the Gospel, they do not enjoy the warrant of biblical truth. They are only as commendable as the relevance of their application allows.

This book is not an interpretation of John's Gospel. It does not attempt to say "what John meant." It is a book about theological reflection which is stimulated, prodded, challenged, and shaped by John's Gospel. Consequently some of the classic Johannine themes and assertions will not be very prominent in this study.

This book is not unbiased about theological reflection. After more than fifteen years in the field, I have many convictions about what it is and how it should be done. Despite my best self-critical effort, I'm sure that I will overstate the case at times and find my prejudices verified in the

Gospel — whether they are there or not. The reader must make the necessary corrections.

Finally, while the focus of the book is theological reflection, the interest is wider than that. Observations about ministry, church, pastoral situations, personality types, specific skills, allies, and troublemakers will inevitably sneak in. My intention is to keep them marginal to the main focus.

Because I am presenting John's Gospel in response to my agenda, I do not follow the traditional order of the chapters. After an initial chapter in which I describe the meaning of theological reflection today, I examine John to see what it says about the goal of theological reflection (chapter two) and the obstacles to it (chapter three). Next I consider theological reflection during a one-to-one encounter (chapter four) and in a group discussion (chapter five). Then I discuss the action outcome of theological reflection (chapter six) and the nature of theological reflection as a continuous process (chapter seven). I conclude with a reflection on the prologue of the Gospel. By the end I have shaped a cumulative picture of theological reflection which I hope will be helpful to those who reflect on their experience today, a task envisioned by the pastoral revolutionaries of thirty-five years ago — and by the author of John's Gospel long before that.

CHAPTER I

What Is
Theological Reflection?

The term *theological reflection* is not very revealing; in fact, it's somewhat redundant. To grasp its meaning one must look at its background. For the specific purpose of this book (pastoral training for ministry) there are two important influences.

CLINICAL PASTORAL EDUCATION

The Clinical Pastoral Education (CPE) movement began in the United States in the 1920s. A few pastoral trainers (Anton Boisen, William Keller, Richard Cabot) simultaneously though independently began to use the clinical experience of students in hospitals and social agencies to teach them the skills of pastoral care.

After some early struggles within the movement and with existing seminary programs, this clinical approach became an accepted part of Protestant seminary preparation, and the formation of the Association for Clinical Pastoral Education (1967) enhanced its professional status and solidified the standards for clinical pastoral training.

In the mid-1950s several advocates of CPE (Helen Flanders Dunbar, Seward Hiltner, Carroll Wise) began to stress the theological potential of clinical education. When the Roman Catholic Church reoriented its seminary program after Vatican II with a more pastoral emphasis, many Catholic seminaries in the United States adopted the prevailing CPE model and adapted it to accommodate the traditional goal of spiritual and theological formation of priests.

The entry of Catholic seminaries into clinical education reinforced the role of theology in clinical training just when Protestant pastoral theologians were making the same appeal. The common quest of Catholic and Protestant seminaries to draw theology from pastoral practice has shaped the goals of theological field education as well as clinical pastoral education and created a significant, though often overlooked, ecumenical achievement in the pastoral field.

LIBERATION THEOLOGY

The second influence on theological reflection is the liberation theology movement, especially as practiced in small Christian communities in Latin America and increasingly in the United States. What began as a method for adult literacy turned into a theological revolution when people started reflecting on the socio-economic conditions of their lives in light of the Bible, worship, and popular devotions and discovered new meanings in these traditional sources.

The interpretation of theology by the experience of the

poor was a sharp reversal of the established theological method. It shared with CPE the starting point of current experience and the search for theological meaning within it, but it went beyond CPE with a more critical interpretation of the theological tradition itself and a more structural emphasis on the action which should result from reflection.

This twofold thrust of Latin American liberation theology could not be kept at a cultural distance. As African-Americans and women in the United States began reflecting on their experience, they too formulated critical interpretations of theology and pressed for a praxis of structural change. The impact of their agenda was felt by CPE although these two movements have for the most part developed independently of each other. Nonetheless they share the common characteristics of beginning with the actual events or circumstances of current life, examining them critically in light of faith, and letting this critical reflection lead to consistent action (praxis). That process has come to be called theological reflection.

THEOLOGICAL REFLECTION

Within the realm of pastoral training, theological reflection refers to a process of learning which begins with one's own experience of ministering. The ministry is ordinarily specified by a contract and carried out in a field placement with supervision on-site and/or at the school. Thus the ministry occurs within a structured, supervised program of seminary field education (also true for the Doctor of Ministry degree) or CPE training in freestanding institutions.

In these settings the minister is usually also engaged

in an academic study of theology. As a result theological reflection is often thought of as the correlation of course work with field experience. It need not be limited to this. A person's whole theological and ministerial background is utilized in theological reflection. This is especially true regarding personal faith convictions and the spiritual insight gained from prayer, discussion, and living out of religious beliefs.

When theological reflection occurs in the structured setting of a pastoral program, students form peer groups, under the guidance of a supervisor (from the faculty or staff). Often theological reflection is not the only, or even the primary, goal of the group. Other issues like skill development, pastoral style, and personal maturation are also on the agenda. Occasionally group discussions are held for the sole purpose of reflecting theologically on a student's experience in ministry, but most of the time theological reflection has to compete for its share of the session.

In the typical format of a peer group discussion one of the members presents an incident. The incident is intended to give the group a glimpse of the student's ministry and raise issues worth reflecting on. The reflection may focus on theological topics as well as the student's ministerial skill or personal development.

There is no single method, or even set of questions, which all theological reflection follows. For the purpose of this book, I am assuming that theological reflection has the following objectives. (1) To *recognize* God's presence in the particular event which the student presents. Theological reflection presumes that God is present in every event and relies on the student to select an event which promises to reveal God in a new or challenging or profound way. (2) To *relate* this recognition of God's presence to one's previous knowledge about God (theology). Theological reflection respects the wisdom and insight of tradition while remaining open to, indeed encouraging, new avenues of thought and new glimpses of the divine truth. (3) To *enact* the theological meaning which has been discovered. If a meaningful experience is creatively reflected upon, it will call for some further expression. Theological reflection expects and encourages this.

In general theological reflection presumes that God is present and active in every event and seeks to recognize that presence and let it lead to both theological and ministerial conclusions. Yet what does this have to do with John's Gospel?

JOHN'S GOSPEL

The overall style of John's Gospel resembles the event-reflection-action approach of theological reflection. In contrast to the synoptic Gospels, John often presents a more developed theological interpretation of events which in turn suggests the praxis of the Christians for whom the Gospel was written. Some examples will make this clear.

Cleansing the Temple (2:13-22)   Jesus acts first, clearing the merchants and money changers out of the temple precincts, then he engages in a theological interpretation of his action with "the Jews." The praxis of this passage is not expressed in the Gospel incident itself, but points to the Gospel's climax where the temple of Jesus' body is destroyed and raised up by God.

Woman at the Well (4:4-42)   Jesus engages a Samaritan woman during her routine task of drawing water. From this simple beginning, he reflects with her on the spiritual meaning of water (a reference to Christian baptism) and worship. Their discussion leads to the recognition that he is the Messiah. The woman puts this into practice by telling the villagers about Jesus and bringing them to him.

Sabbath Cure (5:1-15)   Jesus heals a man who had been sick a long time. Because the healing took place in violation of the sabbath custom, a discussion arises about healing on the sabbath which in turn opens up a larger discussion between Jesus and "the Jews" about his claims for doing these things — a kind of praxis of self-disclosure.

Feeding the Multitude (6:1-71)   Jesus feeds the multitude who had been following him and the next day begins to reflect on the image of the bread of life, equating himself with the bread which comes down from heaven. The praxis which follows is very divisive, with many of the disciples leaving him because of his enacting the reflection.

Man Born Blind (9:1-41)   Jesus cures a man born blind and the event touches off a heated reflection about who did it, how it was done, whether it was valid, and what it meant. The praxis which results is the man's expulsion from the synagogue and Jesus' re-entry into the man's life, leading to his acceptance of Jesus as the Son of man.

Raising of Lazarus (11:1-44)   Jesus delays going to visit his sick friend, Lazarus. When he finally arrives, Lazarus is already dead. This prompts a theological reflection with Martha on belief in the resurrection which leads in turn, through Mary, to the praxis of raising Lazarus from the dead.

Washing the Disciples' Feet (13:1-17) Jesus begins his last supper by washing the feet of his disciples. He then interprets this action and commissions his disciples to enact it in their own lives.

Dialogue with Pilate (18:28–19:16) Jesus is arrested and brought before Pilate. They begin a reflection on the meaning of power and kingship. The praxis that results is that Pilate abdicates his type of power and Jesus enacts his.

Resurrection Appearances (20–21) Jesus makes unexpected appearances to Mary Magdalene, the disciples, Thomas, and (in a later addition to the text) the disciples at the Sea of Tiberias. Each of these events is accompanied by a specific insight into the meaning of his resurrection. The praxis is common in all these appearances: believe and spread the word.

The structure of these episodes suggests a kinship between the Gospel of John and theological reflection. The goal of this book is to examine the Gospel more closely in order to draw some guidance for doing theological reflection today (keeping in mind the provisos listed in the introduction). The hope is not just to verify what contemporary theological reflectors seek to do, but to enhance it with the help of John.

CHAPTER 2

The Goal of
Theological Reflection

Theological reflection seeks to recognize the divine presence in the events of life and to shape subsequent events in light of that recognition. This is different from the customary goal of learning theology by studying the sources of religious belief (e.g., the Bible, worship, doctrine) and the body of opinion which these sources have generated (e.g., biblical theology, systematic theology, moral theology).

In contrast to the academic study of theology, theological reflection is more like spiritual discernment. It is a faith-inspired examination, a search for God's presence in the episodes which constitute a person's experience.

Theological reflection presumes that there *is* a divine presence in these events. It does not insert God into "merely human" events or make God-less incidents theological by describing them in theological terms or using them to introduce a theological lesson. Theological reflection tries to recognize the divine presence inherent in human events and to let that presence illuminate familiar theological terms and lessons.

Of course, in order to recognize the divine presence, a person should have some idea of what it is. This may come from many sources, including previously acquired (academic) theological knowledge. Theological reflection is not opposed to this theological learning. It draws upon it and contributes to it by adding its own distinctive perspective.

The interaction between theological reflection and theological learning is increased when a group reflects on a particular event. A group not only brings a variety of perspectives but also has a greater accumulation of knowledge and insight than an individual does. Members of a group can sometimes recognize God's presence in a person's life more quickly, clearly, or accurately than the person can. In fact, sometimes a person might miss God's presence altogether without others to point it out.

This goal of recognizing God's presence, especially with the help of others, occurs at the beginning of the Gospel of John. It contains some valuable lessons for theological reflection.

JOHN THE BAPTIZER

"There is one among you whom you do not recognize — the one who is to come after me — the strap of whose sandal I am not worthy to unfasten" (1:26-27). John the Baptizer's testimony is the credo of theological reflection. The divine presence is among us but we do not recognize it. Our attention is drawn to the immediate, sensory data of things and our reflection is channeled into observations, interpretations, judgments, insights, and testimonies about what we perceive. But this does not let us get close enough even to unfasten a sandal strap because the divine presence is not just one of these many things among us. It permeates everything and requires a different kind of seeing, an in-sight into the meaning of what is in our midst, an insight that changes the very things we see.

"The next day, when John caught sight of Jesus coming toward him, he exclaimed: 'Look! There is the Lamb of God who takes away the sin of the world' " (1:29). How did John know? Was he blessed with special prophet's eyes not given to ordinary folk? Apparently not. "I confess I did not recognize him, though the very reason I came baptizing with water was that he might be revealed to Israel" (1:31).

This is a great consolation for those who do theological reflection. If John, whose mission was to reveal Jesus, did not recognize him, then perhaps teachers and students, supervisors and trainers, theologians and ministers might expect to have a little difficulty recognizing him too. (Of course, the author of John's Gospel was setting up a contrast between the Baptizer and the Beloved Disciple, whose teachings inspired the Gospel and who always showed greater recognition of Jesus than any of the others.)

How did John finally come to recognize Jesus? He made connections. He combined the stirrings of the one who sent him to baptize with his knowledge of what the prophets had said and his encounters with penitents and skeptics. "The one who sent me to baptize with water told me, 'When you see the Spirit descend and rest on someone, it is he who is to baptize with the Holy Spirit' " (1:33). We may be tricked by artists' renderings of Jesus' baptism into thinking John was to keep his eyes open for a large bird to hover over this someone. If so, there is no excuse for John's not recognizing Jesus. Yet the meaning is surely more subtle.

John realized that when he met someone whose speech

and action showed that a special Spirit was at work, that's the one he should recognize as the Spirit baptizer. To ordinary sight, this person would be one more face in the crowd, another body in line at the Jordan. Even for John's eyes it would take time and several sightings before he would recognize that the one the Spirit was resting on was Jesus of Nazareth.

Like those who do theological reflection, John had to take in a lot, ponder it, connect it to what he already knew, test it, measure himself by it, pray over it, acknowledge his prior oversights, learn from them, think it all through again, and decide. Slow work. His recognition was not a spontaneous, self-evident affirmation made in the first two minutes of meeting Jesus. It came gradually because it was imbedded in such familiar surroundings. Perhaps this was why John had difficulty recognizing Jesus at first — he was so similar to the others, so inconspicuous.

Theological reflectors face the same challenge when they try to recognize the divine presence in the events of their lives. This presence rarely leaps out unmistakably. It moves comfortably among the people and actions and feelings of ordinary experience, almost in camouflage. To recognize it requires paying attention to what's going on, recalling past interpretations, checking interior feelings and urges.

Even when reflectors set out to find the divine presence in their experience, they might miss it if their idea of how or where God should appear is too fixed. This is the liability of formal theological learning. It provides concepts and descriptions which appear differently in the comments and activities of ordinary people. You might be looking for a stranger with a dove when it's your neighbor's insight that reveals where the Spirit is resting.

John's testimony reminds all theological reflectors that recognition of the divine presence doesn't come automatically or easily. But it does come, with reflection — and the help of others.

THE BAPTIZER'S DISCIPLES

Immediately after the testimony of John the Baptizer, Jesus began to assemble his disciples. From the evangelist's viewpoint this action anticipates major themes which will be played out in the rest of the Gospel. The passage sets forth a progression of titles from Lamb of God to Rabbi to Messiah to Son of God. Each new disciple advances the recognition and builds a dramatic preview of the gospel story.

From the viewpoint of theological reflection this passage illustrates different ways of recognizing the divine presence and the diverse roles others can play in that process.

The first two disciples "followed the lead" of their instructor. When John pointed out Jesus as the Lamb of God, "the two disciples heard what he said and followed Jesus" (1:37). They did not launch out on their own but followed the direction of their teacher even though it meant leaving the relative security of what they already knew.

Theological reflection entails a similar invitation. The primary instructor is experience itself; the invitation is to follow its lead, often with some coaching from an experienced guide or trusted peers. Sometimes it is only the prompting of another that nudges us out of the comfort zones we establish.

As soon as they started out, however, they were "caught off guard." Jesus turned around and asked them, "What are you looking for?" (1:38). Of course, they didn't know. It wasn't their idea to follow him in the first place, but they had to explain themselves, so they asked an awkward question, innocuous and intimate at the same time. "Where do you stay?" In one sense it made no difference where he stayed. Who he was and what he did were the important questions, but the disciples didn't know how to ask them. Ironically the question they did ask actually invited them into his private life.

The same thing can happen in a theological reflection discussion. One person can raise a question or suggest an opinion without knowing where it will lead, and suddenly members are face-to-face with one another on more personal terms than they intended. In itself this can be a sign that the discussion is really following the lead of the experience and the participants are comfortable with one another. On the other hand the privacy of each person must be respected and no one should be embarrassed by an unexpected turn in the conversation.

Jesus sensed the sincerity of the disciples and perhaps their disorientation. "Come and see," he invited. He didn't require a well-thought-out plan or a predetermined conclusion. He was satisfied that they were willing to follow a lead and let themselves be caught off guard by what they found. The Gospel doesn't tell us exactly what they found, but it was meaningful enough to keep them there the rest of the day (1:39).

Theological reflection works in a similar way. The common search for the divine presence opens up leads, suggests directions, and invites members to follow them, not knowing where they will end up but being willing to enter more deeply into what appears and to stay with it, perhaps all day.

Whatever the disciples learned from their encounter
with Jesus prompted them to share it the next day. One of
them, Andrew, went at once to his brother, Simon, told him
what had happened, and brought him to Jesus. Simon, as
we know, was impulsive, but he also had a mind of his own.
He was no doubt skeptical about his brother's extraordinary
report, "We have found the Messiah," but underneath his
first reaction there might also have been a desire that it be
true, a passing wish that the hopes of his ancestors might
be fulfilled in his own day, that he might be alive to see it
happen. Not exactly bedrock faith but sufficient openness
for Jesus to see a new identity taking shape within him:
"You are Simon, son of John; your name shall be Cephas"
(1:42).

Theological reflection can sometimes propose pre-
posterous speculations but with enough grounding in experience to entice a person to investigate further even if the
first reaction is hesitation or, as in the case of Nathanael,
cynicism.

The story of Andrew and Simon is followed by the
parallel story of Philip and Nathanael. In this case, however,
Jesus came directly to Philip without the Baptizer's media-
tion, and he startled him just as he did Andrew with the
invitation, "Follow me" (1:43). Philip's following is not described (as Andrew's was), but it had the same effect, for
the first thing Philip did was to seek out Nathanael to share
his enthusiasm. "We have found the one Moses spoke of in
the Law — the prophets too." Then he went too far, he
added too many details. "Jesus, son of Joseph, from
Nazareth" (1:45).

In John's Gospel Jesus' human origins are often a stum-
bling block for many of his listeners and would-be disciples.
Nathanael anticipates their reaction. "Can anything good

come from Nazareth?" (1:47). Philip was not dissuaded. "Come, see for yourself."

In a theological reflection group one member can sometimes get carried away with the excitement of a new insight or experience. It helps to have other members who can temper enthusiasm when it gets in the way of seeing what is really there. Sometimes this is done as brusquely as Nathanael's dismissal of Philip's eagerness. The common search for the divine presence can break down at that point. It can be recovered by responding as Philip did: come, see for yourself; look at the experience on your terms, with your eyes; see if you find the same thing.

Nathanael went. Either he respected Philip very much or he harbored the same fragile hope as Peter inside his gruff exterior. Perhaps both, but he would have to be convinced. Jesus met him head-on and praised his resistance to gullibility. "This man is a true Israelite. There is no guile in him" (1:48).

Nathanael heard the compliment in Jesus' greeting, an implicit affirmation that the expectation of the Messiah was too important to be bestowed on every fresh preacher in the valley. Claims had to be examined, impressions had to be tested, truth had to prevail (a dominant theme in John). Jesus was up to the challenge. "Before Philip called you, I saw you under the fig tree" (1:48).

The impression is that Jesus was clairvoyant, eavesdropping on the encounter between Philip and Nathanael. A more realistic interpretation might be that Jesus had had his eye on Nathanael all along, and now that they were face-to-face Jesus could tell him what he had seen in him (just as he looked into Simon and saw the rock core of Peter). Nathanael, the apparent skeptic, recognized by Jesus, in turn recognizes him with the titles which will bring the

Gospel to its climax: "You are the Son of God; you are the king of Israel" (1:49).

The same thing happens when theological reflection is successful. Participants feel almost simultaneously that in recognizing the divine presence in their midst, they are being recognized as well. And this mutual recognition changes them and opens them to new experiences. "Do you believe just because I told you I saw you under the fig tree? You will see much greater things than that" (1:50).

This prediction was verified in the experiences of the Johannine community and gave rise to the distinctive Gospel which they produced. Less dramatically, but no less really, the same expectation guides theological reflection. Every insight, every recognition opens people to see what is present. Theological reflection follows leads (as Andrew and the other disciple did); it pays attention to the deep cravings of the heart (like Peter's) and startling messages (like Philip's), but it does so with a questioning, critical, and sometimes skeptical mind (like Nathanael's).

The example of the disciples depicts the recognition of the divine presence in positive, exciting encounters, but life has other moments — stressful, painful, lonely. In John's Gospel these too can lead to divine recognition.

ROYAL OFFICIAL

Jesus had returned to Cana, and news of his intervention at the wedding party (narrated in chapter two) as well as his deeds in Jerusalem must have been circulating. At least, that's how the Gospel leads into the story of the royal official (4:46). This man came to Jesus out of acute need

— his son was dying. He heard that Jesus was back in Galilee, and he sought him out to ask that he heal his son (4:47).

Jesus' initial response seems a little harsh, even judgmental — the kind of reaction an overworked minister might give to one more request. "Unless you people see signs and wonders, you do not believe" (4:48). Perhaps the edge on Jesus' comment was honed by the opposition he was getting from his own people (already suggested in 2:8-20 and 3:1-21) in contrast to the acceptance by the Samaritans (narrated in 4:39-43). This was probably also the sentiment of the Johannine community put into the mouth of Jesus, as if he anticipated the resistance they would face from their own people.

In any event the official was not deterred. "Sir, come down before my child dies" (4:49). The man drove home the urgency of the situation, and with it his sincerity. He was not looking for more signs; he was not trying to use Jesus (or his son's illness) to draw attention to himself. He was desperate and he looked to Jesus for help.

Jesus in turn recognized his faith (as he had recognized Nathanael's) and gave the man a chance to act on it. "Go your way; your son lives" (4:50). Anyone looking for a display of miraculous power would be dissatisfied with this response, but the man "believed the word Jesus spoke and went off."

The goal of theological reflection is not discussion for its own sake, much less impressing others with personal knowledge. The goal is to recognize the divine presence in a particular situation and to respond to it. This often entails a willingness to act faithfully, without having all the questions answered. In fact, sometimes it is only by acting in faith first that theological insight emerges.

As the man was going home, his servants met him with the good news that his son had recovered. When he asked at what hour he began to show improvement, he learned it was precisely when Jesus told him, "Your son lives." His faith confirmed by this fact, he and his household thereafter believed in Jesus (4:53).

The starting point of theological reflection is human experience. Few experiences are as acute as personal need, and few personal needs are as compelling as parents' concern for their children. Parents are solely responsible for bringing new life into the world, but they cannot be solely capable of caring for their children. Sickness is a prime example. Parents, faced with the limits of their own power, look to others for assistance.

How does their looking help them recognize the divine presence? In the case of the royal official, all concern was for the child. He did not invoke his status and expect Jesus to come to him; he sought Jesus out. He did not insist on being in charge (as he usually was in his job) but he acknowledged his dependency publicly. He did not use his wealth to "get the best help money could buy" but he let his need speak for itself. He was not put off by Jesus' critique of "people like him" who want assurances first, and he did not balk when Jesus gave him no more than his word that his son would recover.

The royal official was able to do all this because his concern for his son was paramount and he believed Jesus could help. The role of theological reflection in such a situation is similar — to focus on the welfare of those in need and to act on the level of faith they bring to the situation. Ministers can help people do this to the extent they themselves have learned to do it, and a theological reflection group is one of the best places to learn it.

MARY MAGDALENE

Need of a different sort affected Mary Magdalene. Her need had come about through loss, specifically the loss of Jesus through death. In her grief she went to the last place she had seen him, the tomb, "while it was still dark" (20:1). The light which had come into the world seemed to be extinguished, and the darkness which appears so prominently in John's symbolism seemed to reign.

Mary must have been experiencing the typical emotions of grief intensified by the suddenness of Jesus' execution. The Gospel doesn't indicate what she expected to find when she went to the tomb, but she certainly didn't expect to find it empty. Her first reaction was confusion and a spontaneous return to her companions: "She ran off to Simon Peter and the other disciple (the one Jesus loved) and told them, 'The Lord has been taken from the tomb! We don't know where they have put him'" (20:2).

Mary tried to make sense of what she had observed, but it only seemed to increase her distress. The other disciples weren't much more enlightened (although the Gospel credits the beloved disciple with "believing" when he entered the empty tomb [20:9], an unprecedented event which looks like the Gospel's attempt to enhance its hero).

Sometimes theological reflection draws blanks. Available interpretations don't seem to fit the experience; suggestions from others might shed no light and might even complicate things. A person can feel alone and empty, like Mary.

Left by the men who went back home, unable to figure things out for herself, Mary stayed at the scene and continued to gaze and peer and try to see. Her sorrow was reflected back to her through two angels whose question, "Why are you weeping?" forced her to declare her loss and helplessness. "Because the Lord has been taken away, and I do not know where they have put him" (20:13). As with so many mourners who experience only the absence of the beloved, Mary's vision was blocked.

"She had no sooner said this than she turned around and caught sight of Jesus standing there. But she did not know him" (20:14). Like John the Baptizer, Mary does not recognize the very one she is looking for; her previous experience of him and her present desires are not adequate for the divine presence now in her midst.

Her grief causes her to hear only the repeated question, not the person asking: "Why are you weeping? Who is it you are looking for?" (20:15). She responds at her level of recognition. "Sir, if you are the one who carried him off, tell me where you have laid him and I will take him away." Even a corpse is preferable to the dark silence and emptiness of the tomb. Like the royal official, desperate for any response, she waits.

Sometimes the contribution of theological reflection is not a solution to a specific problem but a strategy, a way of staying with a situation, of feeling it, of making it one's own, of letting it speak a word never heard before.

"Mary." In the silence of her reflection she felt this experience as hers; it was addressing her, inviting her to let something unimagined occur, something that no outsider could share or describe. Mary could not recognize the Lord until she allowed herself to be changed by the situation itself.

Theological reflection can help this process by withholding familiar explanations that don't really fit and letting the novelty of an experience speak for itself. This is especially true in very powerful or overwhelming experiences — like the death of a loved one. Although the recognition of the Lord within the experience is directly available only to the one affected, the results of the recognition can and should be shared.

"Go to my brothers and tell them, 'I am ascending to my Father and your Father, to my God and your God!'" (20:17). In contrast to her previous visit to the disciples when she was confused and desperate, Mary now approaches them with clarity and purpose: "I have seen the Lord!" (20:19). Her story of recognition is not theirs, but it will help them recognize the same Lord in their own experiences.

Theological reflection requires a personal involvement in the experience being reflected upon. This is especially true for experiences of death and grief. At first, such reflection can seem distressing and suggest a dependency on others, as if they can see what you cannot.

As long as reflectors stay outside the emotional trauma and try to make sense of it in terms of what they already know, they are not likely to come to any recognition. Theological reflection tries to open people to new encounters by following their initial reactions and interpretations to the divine presence waiting to be recognized. Of course, the Lord does not wait passively as the following incident shows.

THE DISCIPLES ON THE SEA

In John's Gospel there are two accounts of the disciples recognizing Jesus while at sea. Each time, a major theological event precedes the encounter. The first comes after Jesus' feeding of the multitude (6:16-22). The second occurs after Jesus' resurrection (21:1-14). They may be one incident retold in two versions. Taken together, they offer some helpful lessons about theological reflection.

After feeding the multitude, Jesus fled to the mountain when he sensed the people wanted to "carry him off to make him king" (6:15). The disciples waited for him, but when he didn't return and it became dark, they started sailing toward Capernaum without him.

In the post-resurrection story, seven of the disciples were on the shore of the Sea of Tiberias and Peter suddenly announced that he was going fishing. The others went along and fished unsuccessfully through the night.

In both of these accounts the disciples are alone, darkness surrounds them, and they are engaged in ordinary, familiar activities — sailing and fishing. Indeed, these are not unlike the settings in which many people begin theological reflection — ordinary events, a solitary moment, no clear vision of Jesus. Things change when Jesus takes initiative.

In the first episode a strong wind came up and the sea became rough. Just then the disciples caught sight of Jesus walking toward them on the water. They recognized him but were frightened by what they saw, so he reassured them: "It is I; do not be afraid" (6:20).

In the second episode Jesus was standing on the shore but the disciples did not recognize him. He initiated a discussion. "Children, have you caught anything to eat?" (21:5). When they said they had not, he told them to cast their net off the starboard side and they would. They did. Then the beloved disciple recognized Jesus and informed Peter (the customary pattern in John), who immediately jumped in the water and swam to shore.

In both situations Jesus appears unexpectedly. He simply shows up in the midst of the disciples' activity. Once he is recognized, everything turns toward him. He becomes the focus of attention and the drawing power of their experience.

In the first story the disciples "wanted to take him into the boat but suddenly it came aground on the shore they had been approaching" (6:21). It was as if their recognition of him brought them to the very place they had been struggling to reach on their own.

In the second story the disciples brought their catch of fish to a shore which was suddenly not so far out — "they were not far from land, no more than a hundred yards" (21:8). As they drew closer, they saw that Jesus had already prepared a fire and had placed a fish on it, but he wanted some of theirs as well.

In both stories Jesus completes the disciples' efforts. As soon as they are in contact with him, their goal is reached. They are already aground; they are really not far from the shore — and breakfast. But there is more. Their recognition of Jesus leads to a deeper union with him. In the first account this is actualized through his teaching on the bread of life; in the second account through his feeding them.

What do these stories teach about theological reflection? Much theological reflection dwells on ordinary events, but these events occur against the backdrop of all the other events in a person's life and emerge out of these prior events. This cumulative background often enables a person to see the divine presence in current, ordinary events.

The influence of explicitly religious or spiritual experience is especially strong in this regard. Both the feeding of the multitude and the feeding of the disciples have a eucharistic character which creates the climate in which the disciples recognize Jesus. Similarly, reflectors' participation in worship and formal prayer cultivates a sense of God's presence which accompanies them in the routine activities of daily life. The connections may not appear as dramatically as Jesus walking on water or calling instructions from the shore, but the continuity of experiences facilitates the power of recognition.

Theological reflection tries to foster this interplay. It focuses on ordinary events but encourages reflectors to view them with their whole selves, to draw upon those previous moments when they have sensed deeply the presence of the Lord, especially at prayer or worship. Using these pieces of one's own history and listening to others do the same can bring reflectors ashore before they know it and help them realize how unthinkable it is to go anywhere else for their nourishment.

SUMMARY

The goal of theological reflection is to recognize the divine presence in the events of human life. John's Gospel offers the following reminders relative to this goal.

1. Recognizing the divine presence is not easy or automatic even when your intention is to discover it.

2. The divine presence is usually recognized gradually, by making connections between current and past events; personal experience and tradition; your own insights and the observations of others; critical thinking and imagination.

3. People recognize the divine presence with the help of one another: by following the lead of instructors, by responding to the initiatives of peers, by letting the reflection process open new possibilities.

4. An experience of need, especially the feeling of powerlessness in trying to help another person, is a prime occasion for recognizing the divine presence.

5. The experience of grief can reveal the divine presence

if a person is willing to enter the pain of loss and let go of customary ways of recognizing God's presence.

6. The ability to recognize the divine presence is cumulative; previous encounters, especially in prayer and worship, increase your ability to recognize the divine presence even when it occurs in unexpected ways.

CHAPTER 3

Obstacles to Theological Reflection

The goal of theological reflection is to recognize the divine presence in the events of daily life. As described in the last chapter, this is not a simple, quick, or automatic process. A person who is consciously looking for the divine presence (like John the Baptizer) might not recognize it. Reflectors who are open to the lead of others (as John's disciples were) might not know what they're looking for. Those who do have a definite idea of what they're looking for (like the royal official or Mary Magdalene) may find that the divine presence appears in unexpected ways. People may feel at sea (like Jesus' disciples) simply waiting for the divine presence to emerge.

In one sense these difficulties are to be expected; they reflect the humanness of the search and lend a natural, sometimes humorous, touch to the task of theological reflection. In themselves these human limitations are not really obstacles; they are part of the process of theological reflection.

Obstacles to theological reflection are barriers which

needn't exist. They arise from an unwillingness to do what theological reflection requires. Usually this means an un-willingness to be led by experience and to learn from what is happening. Students and teachers of theology must be aware of this obstacle because they tend to become so im-mersed in an academic, scientific form of theology that they measure every theological claim by this standard. As a result, they can close themselves off from a rich source of theolog-ical insight and unnecessarily narrow their theological vi-sion.

Obstacles of this type must have been a major concern to the Johannine community because they appear so frequently in the Gospel itself. By examining them in their own context, one can draw some helpful applications for theological reflection. To make the applications more perti-nent, the obstacles will be described as reliance on external authority, lack of imagination, and self-protection.

RELIANCE ON EXTERNAL AUTHORITY

This obstacle arises most often in Jesus' disputes with the religious authorities. The following four incidents are worth looking at.

Cleansing of the Temple

The cleansing of the temple (2:13-22) may have been the debut Jesus himself had planned and the reason he balked at his mother's request to help the married couple at the wedding feast in Cana (2:4). In any event Jesus certainly acted decisively when he entered the temple.

In the holy city, Jerusalem, at the holy season, Passover, Jesus restored the aura of holiness which had been crowded out of the temple. His action was so forceful that it prompted his disciples to venture an initial theological reflection. As often happens in theological reflection, a significant event suggests a biblical passage: "Zeal for your house consumes me" (2:17). The disciples saw Jesus illustrating this passage, bringing it dramatically to life through his deeds.

Even "the Jews" who immediately confronted him did not question the need for a cleansing or the appropriateness of restoring a spiritual atmosphere to the temple precincts (2:18). The praxis was justified, the practitioner was not. "What sign can you show us authorizing you to do these things?" Their primary concern was of secondary importance, for they were concerned with external authority rather than internal authenticity. Jesus wasn't very helpful.

"Destroy this temple and in three days I will raise it up" (2:19). His antagonists could not follow the meaning of this symbolic statement. Jesus was pointing them from the temple of stone and wood and glass to the temple of his flesh and blood and eventually to the spiritual temple of a new body, the community of his disciples. But they never got out of the temple precincts, staggered by the apparent absurdity of his claim to do in three days what their ancestors had done in forty-six years.

The disciples were not much more enlightened at the time, but after Jesus' resurrection they recalled what he said. A new experience triggered their recollection and clarified the meaning of the previous event. This is how theological reflection often works. Each experience speaks for itself; reflection links them together and tries to recognize the meaning which has been imbedded in them all the time. This kind of reflection succeeds when it helps people, as it helped the disciples "come to believe the Scripture and the word he had spoken" (2:22).

Relying on external authority is an obstacle to this process, and sometimes, as in this case, to Jesus himself. Jesus declared that the authority for his action was in the act itself because it allowed the glory and reign of God to be manifested. The God who acted through him was his authority, and that God should have been recognizable in the signs that Jesus performed. Pay attention to the experience, Jesus might have said; it speaks clearly enough. Don't be distracted by who is doing it or when and where it is being done (lessons he himself may have learned at Cana).

What does this episode say about theological reflection? "The Jews" (a sort of critical reflection group for Jesus) were too quick to move away from the experience. They had to measure it by their own standards (who has authority, who can give permission), but as soon as they did that, they lost the meaning of the experience and their opportunity to learn from it. The same temptation faces theological reflectors, especially when an experience is disturbing or threatening. Instead of letting the experience help them discover what may be learned, theological reflectors can raise questions about who is qualified to say what it means and by which "objective" criteria they may speak.

Theological reflection trusts experience. It is an obstacle to this trust to resort too quickly or too confidently to external authority. The cleansing of the temple was not the only time this obstacle arose.

Cure at Bethesda

Chapter five of John's Gospel is written as if it were a theological reflection paper. First, an act of ministry is described with verbatim exchanges (5:1-15); then, a reflection on the event is presented (5:16-47).

The occasion was a Jewish feast, and Jesus was in Jerusalem to celebrate it. The narrator sketches the setting factually (as the presenter of a ministerial experience might): the place was called Bethesda near the Sheep Pool where the blind, lame, or disabled would gather. Among them was one man who had been sick for thirty-eight years (5:2-5).

Jesus came on the scene (as a minister might enter a hospital). He wasted no time, knowing that the man had been sick so long. "Do you want to be healed?" (5:6). It is not clear in what sense Jesus meant this: healed physically or healed spiritually? The former is suggested by the man's condition; the latter by Jesus' ministry in John's Gospel and his comments at the end of this episode. The man responded indirectly, explaining (almost defending) why he had not been healed before now.

"I do not have anyone to plunge me into the pool once the water has been stirred up. By the time I get there, someone else has gone in ahead of me" (5:7). Jesus was not interested in a more complete explanation; he acted quickly and decisively. "Stand up! Pick up your mat and walk!" (5:8). His healing commands worked. "The man was immediately cured; he picked up his mat and began to walk" (5:9).

Jesus responded to the man's immediate need, one of the first instincts of a minister. But he responded in a way that few ministers would be able to imitate — an immediate physical cure. Underneath this dramatic healing, however, lies a lesson that is applicable to all ministers.

Jesus may have sensed the man's overdependence on others to help him out of his predicament. The man said he hadn't been cured for thirty-eight years because there was no one to take him to the water. Perhaps he never considered alternatives; perhaps he assumed that he had no resources of his own which could yield the same result as the pool of water lying before him. Jesus appealed to the man's inner strength, his power of self-determination, the ability to take charge of himself. There are important pastoral care implications here, but the story moves in a different direction.

"That day was a sabbath" (5:9). This ominous note introduces the concern which some of "the Jews" expressed to the cured man. "It is the sabbath, and you are not allowed to carry that mat around" (5:10). They must have known this man; they should have been moved by his cure even if their concern for sabbath regulations prevented them from rejoicing with him. Yet all they could see was a violation, a disruption of external order.

The man had been cured, but not yet changed. Feeling himself in trouble with the authorities, he shifted the blame. "It was the man who cured me who told me, 'Pick up your mat and walk'" (5:11). When pressed for a name, he had no idea who had healed him (neither will the blind man in chapter nine). Apparently the commotion after his cure allowed Jesus "to slip away" (not a bad recommendation for a minister who has just helped someone gain independence).

Still, Jesus wasn't finished. Later he found the man in the temple precincts (which he had purified, in 2:13-16, restoring to them their spiritual character). Jesus now took up his agenda, having satisfied the man's. "Give up your sins so that something worse may not overtake you" (5:14). This was probably the healing Jesus initially wanted to offer the man, but he couldn't get to this level without moving through the physical ailment first — just the sort of stubborn reality that shapes most ministry.

Where does this episode lead theologically? For "the Jews" there were two issues: the violation of the sabbath and

Jesus' "speaking of God as his own Father, thereby making himself God's equal" (5:18). The first point related to the cure; the second to the growing reputation of Jesus. The first concern led into the second (just as a presenting problem in ministry is often the prelude to something else, not directly related but of more importance).

Jesus kept the two issues connected. He responded to the sabbath objection by saying, "My Father is at work until now, and I am at work as well" (5:17). God is not controlled by the sabbath, nor is the one who does God's work. Jesus carried the comparison further, invoking the way a son learns from his father by watching him work, as Jesus must have watched and learned from Joseph.

"The Son cannot do anything by himself — he can do only what he sees the Father doing" (5:19) and "The Father loves the Son and everything the Father does he shows him" (5:20). This homey example suggests that anyone who "watches" the Father, who is attuned to God's ways after generations of instruction, should at least be able to recognize God's work in Jesus' ministry. Yet God's work is not recognized when those watching are preoccupied with external authorization.

If such an obstacle prevents them from seeing the meaning of this cure, it will also prevent them from seeing greater works than making a man mobile. "Just as the Father raises the dead and grants life, so the Son grants life to those to whom he wishes" (5:21). The experience of seeing the lame man stand up, pick up his mat, and begin to walk must have stimulated Jesus' imagination to envision the dead rising to life. And in the apocalyptic atmosphere of the time, resurrection entailed judgment.

"The Father himself judges no one, but has assigned all judgment to the Son" (5:22). But the Son does not judge from a distance, as an external authority. The Son *is* judgment, acting within events and from this position providing their interpretation. Those who believe in him are thereby judged righteous and possess eternal life, whereas those who do not believe in him are condemned by their very disbelief. The truth of this assertion depends on the union of the Son and the Father and the ability of people to see in the Son's deeds the work of God (5:24-30).

Jesus appealed to the testimony contained within the works he performed, just as theological reflection appeals to the truth contained within the experiences it investigates. This approach walks a fine line between claiming a wholly self-contained authority and relying wholly on an external, disconnected authority. "The Jews" were right to be concerned. The self-serving claims of many pretenders had already threatened the sovereignty of God. But new claims should be tested on their own merits, not on assumptions drawn from the authority of the past.

Jesus did not ask people to accept his word unquestioningly. He asked them to hear God's word in his, to recognize God's deeds in his works. Then they would know that "there is another who is testifying on my behalf" (5:32). External authority should not substitute for the testimony Jesus had in mind. Even someone as great, and acceptable, as John the Baptizer was not equal to the testimony of the works Jesus performed. The scriptures themselves, "in which you think you have eternal life" (5:39), only lead to that life which the Father gives through Jesus.

Similarly, theological reflection is not accomplished merely by citing the opinions of respected theologians or listing pertinent scriptural passages. These resources can lead reflectors to the life vibrating within the experience; they should not take the place of that life. It is not enough to have theology in your head if "you do not have the love of God in your hearts" (5:42).

It is this contact with the living God that made the difference for Jesus. "I have come in my Father's name, yet you do not accept me. But let someone come in his own name and him you will accept" (5:43). And harsher still, "You accept praise from one another yet do not seek the glory that comes from God" (5:44).

This is a severe warning for theological reflectors. It is tempting to use an experience to expound one's own opinions or those of a favorite theologian. But that is to remain in the condition of the man in this story — too dependent on others to move. The challenge is to let the elements in experience guide reflection. Chapter five of John is an excellent example of what this means.

A good work is performed which prompts Jesus to reflect on the works his Father has given him to do. The cure enables a man to rise up and walk freely; Jesus reflects on the power of God to raise the dead and give them life. The cure is judged harshly because it takes place on the sabbath; Jesus reflects on the place of judgment, who renders it, and what it is about.

Along the way there are references to John the Baptizer, Moses, and the whole of Scripture. There is also a familial illustration of a son imitating what he sees his father doing. There is an acknowledgment of the popular (but not unanimous) conception of resurrection and judgment. There is a comment on the tendency to be impressed by self-seeking public figures, and there is the chilling climax — you do not have the love of God in your hearts.

In a similar way theological reflection draws upon Scripture and theological authorities; uses analogies from human experience; takes into account popular understandings of the faith and cultural influences; and comes face to face with the theological meaning of reflection — to deepen the love of God in our hearts. Too much of this is sacrificed by relying on external authority.

Reliance on external authority was not limited to "the Jews" who held that authority. Jesus faced the same obstacle from his relatives and the crowds of ordinary folk.

Feast of Booths

The threats on Jesus' life (alluded to in 5:18) were becoming serious, so Jesus "moved about within Galilee" rather than in Judea (7:1). But he didn't escape tension. As the Feast of Booths approached, his relatives prodded him, somewhat sarcastically, to do his showing off in Judea. "No one who wishes to be known publicly keeps his actions hidden. If you are going to do things like these, you may as well display yourself to the world at large" (7:4).

Despite Jesus' repeated insistence that he was only doing the works God wanted him to do, those who knew him longest (though not necessarily best) thought he was only promoting himself. Jesus resorted to his sense of timing and desire for a low profile (major Johannine themes). "I am not going up to this festival because the time is not yet ripe for me" (7:9). Of course, he did go — and promptly got into controversy.

Advocates of theological reflection sometimes feel resistance and hear condescending remarks from colleagues. These moments are certainly not on a par with the opposition Jesus faced, but they can come from a mentality which relies too much on external authority.

Even before his arrival, people were looking for Jesus and trading their opinions about him. "Where is that troublemaker?" "He is a good man." "Not at all — he is only misleading the crowd" (7:11-12). These exchanges were private, "for fear of the Jews" whose threats against Jesus were apparently taken very seriously and were thought to extend to anyone who even talked about him in public. (This is also likely a reflection of the Johannine community's experience, because the people in this incident actually do speak quite openly with and about Jesus.)

It is unthinkable that anyone would face a death threat for advocating theological reflection, at least in the United States. In other countries, notably in Latin America, many have faced such threats and paid the price for encouraging people to reflect on and act out of their experience. Without going to that extreme, opposition to theological reflection can still create a climate of discomfort and antagonism which has some kinship to the situation of Jesus. He didn't back away.

"The feast was half over by the time Jesus went into the temple area and began to teach" (7:14). The contrast is unmistakable. Whenever the crowds were vociferous, Jesus became silent and even hid. Whenever the crowds were silent, Jesus spoke publicly. His time and their time were not in harmony. His message and their receptiveness were not in phase. This dissonance made some of the people try to explain him away.

"How did this man get his education when he had no teacher?" (7:15). The people assumed that the only reliable path to knowledge of their religious tradition was through the established channels of rabbinic education, just as some today assume that the only reliable path to theological knowledge is an academic degree. Jesus represented an alternative.

"My doctrine is not my own; it comes from him who

sent me. Any man who chooses to do his will will know about this doctrine — namely, whether it comes from God or is simply spoken on my own" (7:16-17). Jesus made the same appeal he had used in defense of his cleansing of the temple and his sabbath cure of the lame man at Bethesda. It was an appeal to the divine genesis within every author-itative religious experience — including the Mosaic Law.

"Moses has given you the law, has he not?" Go within it, Jesus implied, to the core experience which gave rise to it, and you will know what I know. But, "not one of you keeps it." In fact, they wanted to use it to kill the very person whom it revealed. "Why do you look for a chance to kill me?" (7:19).

The crowd rebelled at this suggestion (7:20), but Jesus completed his parallel. Those who were astonished that Jesus cured a lame man on the sabbath would themselves circum-cise a man on the sabbath. They would promote a ritual while letting a person suffer needlessly. Their perception was skewed; their contact with the life of their religion was blocked. "Stop judging by appearances and make an honest judgment" (7:24).

Judging by appearances, from outside a situation, ac-cording to codified learning, is bound to obscure the mean-ing which an experience contains. Jesus did not advocate a wholesale abandonment of religious tradition or deny the value of rabbinic instruction. He counseled that this author-ity remain in living contact with the divine presence revealed here and now. In the same way, theological reflection does not advocate the abandonment of tradition or deny the value of formal learning. Rather it uses tradition and learn-ing to recognize the divine presence in contemporary expe-rience.

Jesus' message caused some to wonder why he wasn't

silenced (7:26); it prompted others to try to seize him (7:30); and it led many to believe in him (7:31). The confusion reached the Pharisees, who, with the chief priests, dispatched the temple guard to get him. It didn't work.

In the second episode during the Feast of Booths, the same divided opinions about Jesus are reported (7:40-44). The temple guards came back empty-handed and explained themselves by saying, "No man ever spoke like that before" (7:46). The Pharisees pulled out all the stops, invoking every external authority they could think of and demeaning everybody in the process. "Do not tell us you too have been taken in! You do not see any of the Sanhedrin believing in him, do you? Or the Pharisees? Only this lot, that knows nothing about the law — and they are lost anyway!" (7:47-49)

The Pharisees were a little presumptuous. At least one of their members, Nicodemus (who had his own obstacle to overcome, as will be seen in the next section), intervened discreetly. "Since when does our law condemn any man without first hearing him and knowing the facts?" (7:51). It was a futile effort. The Pharisees turned on him, using an insult reminiscent of Nathanael's comment about Jesus: "Do not tell us you are a Galilean too." Then they resorted to their primary external authority. "Look it up. You will not find the Prophet coming from Galilee" (7:52).

Insisting on their own authority rather than acknowledging the testimony of Jesus' deeds, the Pharisees tried to use force, claimed more support than they really had, insulted one of their own, and closed themselves off from the possibility of a new, life-giving experience. It wasn't any better when they confronted Jesus directly.

In the third episode during the Feast of Booths, narrated in 8:12-59 after the story of the woman caught in adultery, the Pharisees interrupted Jesus' teaching about light and darkness with the familiar criticism: "You are your own witness. Such testimony cannot be valid" (8:13).

Jesus accepted their accusation and used it to return to his fundamental point. "It is laid down in your law that evidence given by two persons is valid. I am one of those testifying in my behalf, the Father who sent me is the other" (8:18). The Pharisees seemed willing to probe this. "And where is this 'Father' of yours?" (8:19).

Jesus gave them an answer which drew them back into his experience. "If you knew me, you would know my Father too." This certainly must have felt like a vicious circle to those looking for external warrants. They simply could not grasp the meaning, the truth inherent in the situation, as long as they insisted on judging it by appearances, from the outside, with the aid of external authorities. And while they passed judgment, Jesus moved on.

"I am going away. You will look for me but you will die in your sins. Where I am going you cannot come" (8:21). The meaning of experience does not wait, static and time-less. It grows, moves, and changes. It demands a freedom of reflection and interpretation that is consistent with the experience itself. Jesus' listeners showed their ignorance of this by immediately interpreting his statement in the most extreme sense: "Does he mean he will kill himself when he claims, 'Where I am going you cannot come?'" (8:22).

The remainder of chapter eight is a reprise of the themes which have filled these disputes: Jesus' identity and union with the one who sent him (25-26); the authority behind his deeds and teaching (27-29); the appeal to intrin-sic truth (31-32); the use of his opponents' arguments to lead them to his insights (39-41); the accusations and demeaning interpretations put on him (48); the unequivocal assertion that "before Abraham came to be, I AM." (58) The climax of this sequence is not a confession of faith, as with the first disciples (1:35-51), but a preparation for stoning. "At that they picked up rocks to throw at Jesus," but he was already gone (8:59).

What do these disputes teach us about theological reflection? One of the major obstacles to recognizing the divine presence is a reliance on external authority which judges experience by appearance only. To recognize the divine presence, it is necessary to let go of this reliance and to move through the appearances to the actual presence of God. When this happens, the divine presence is its own warrant. That's the insight theological reflection seeks to foster.

Feast of Dedication

During the Feast of Dedication another dispute arose, similar in form and content to those already discussed. In this episode (10:22-38) "the Jews" were getting impatient. They wanted to settle the confusion about Jesus once and for all. "If you really are the Messiah, tell us so in plain words" (10:24). What they meant was, tell us in our words; confirm our preconceptions; fit into what we have already figured out.

The same request in a theological reflection group can take two forms. It can mean that a person wants to discuss experience in abstract theological terms because the ambiguity of experience, the plurality of viewpoints, the diversity of language is too frustrating for one who prefers coherent, systematic thinking. It can also mean that a person doesn't want to think critically or comprehensively, preferring the immunity of "my experience" and "my feelings." The tension between these two approaches can be exasperating.

Jesus was getting impatient too. "I did tell you, but you do not believe me" (10:25). The problem was not with the message but with the listeners. The meaning was plain enough, too plain as a matter of fact. It just wasn't acceptable to those who could not make it fit what they already knew. Using the imagery of the good shepherd, recounted at the beginning of chapter ten, Jesus concluded: "You refuse to believe because you are not my sheep" (10:26).

Jesus' sheep, on the other hand, "hear my voice. I know them and they follow me" (10:27). They are secure in their union with Jesus, and no one shall snatch them out of his hand. That would be equivalent to snatching them out of God's hand, for "the Father and I are one" (10:30).

At that point his listeners picked up stones to throw at him (as they had in 8:59), but he confronted them with his only defense. "Many good deeds have I shown you from the Father. For which of these do you stone me?" (10:33). Of course, it was not for any good deed but for the interpretation he had drawn from those deeds: "you who are only a man are making yourself God" (10:33).

Jesus reminded them that their own law used similar language (10:34-35). The decisive point was not semantics; it was experience. If Jesus performed the works of the Father, let the works speak for themselves. But what the works said to his listeners was, "arrest him."

Those who do theological reflection ultimately have only the assurance of the Good Shepherd's voice. They may not be able to translate that voice convincingly to others and replicate adequately the works which enabled them to hear it. But if they truly hear that voice and keep responding to it, they know they are secure.

LACK OF IMAGINATION

In John's Gospel Jesus usually teaches the same way experience occurs — at different levels simultaneously. This requires from the listener an attentiveness which can move freely among facts, on the alert for meanings revealed only to the imagination and its creative language. Not everyone is willing to think this way, especially if they are trained in a more logical, methodical system — as Nicodemus was.

Nicodemus

Here was a prominent Pharisee, a (minority) member of the Sanhedrin, who gave Jesus the respected title of Rabbi and acknowledged "you are a teacher come from God, for no man can perform signs and wonders such as you perform unless God is with him" (3:2). This was precisely the breakthrough which his colleagues were unable to make (as noted in the previous section). It suggested that Nicodemus was ready for more advanced reflection. But John artfully warns that it's not that easy.

Nicodemus came to Jesus at night. Given the repeated death threats against Jesus in John's Gospel, it made sense that anyone who associated with him would be cautious, even someone of standing like Nicodemus. But the darkness of night is also symbolic in John, indicating in this case that Nicodemus still has a long way to go before he sees the full meaning of the signs and wonders which he has observed Jesus performing.

Jesus' opening comment supports this symbolic view and puts a challenge before Nicodemus. "I solemnly assure you, no one can see the reign of God unless he is begotten from above" (3:3). Typically Jesus responds to the leads

others give him. He starts with their perspective and even
uses their language. Nicodemus spoke of signs; Jesus speaks
of seeing the signs of God's reign. Nicodemus spoke of Jesus
coming from God; Jesus speaks of being begotten from
above.

This is a style theological reflection encourages, especially during the conversations that occur in the ministry.
Ministers should respect experience and accept a situation
the way they find it in order to move with it to a deeper
level of significance. Like some ministers, Nicodemus was
apparently not accustomed to reflecting in this way.

"How can a man be born again once he is old [perhaps
referring to himself]? Can he return to his mother's womb
and be born over again?" (3:4). Not very imaginative;
Nicodemus was stuck on the literal level. Jesus tried again,
alerting Nicodemus that he was speaking spiritually, figura-
tively. He even used the familiar movement of the wind as
a tangible illustration: "The wind blows where it will. You
hear the sound it makes but you do not know where it
comes from, or where it goes. So it is with everyone begotten
of the Spirit" (3:8).

Nicodemus was lost. "How can such a thing happen?"
Jesus was perplexed. "You hold the office of teacher of Israel
and still you do not understand these matters?" So it is with
theological reflection. The signs and wonders of ministry
can be described and analyzed factually or psychologically
or sociologically. But it takes a conversion of thinking to
see their theological meaning. It takes a spiritually attuned
sensitivity which does not come automatically from academic study.

To help Nicodemus (and us) understand, Jesus out-
lined the "proof circle" which he alluded to after cleansing
the temple and reiterated in the disputes with "the Jews"

(analyzed in the previous section). It goes like this: What I say and do comes from my Father with whom I am one. There is no external warrant for my ministry. You will recognize my words and deeds as God's if you know God. And you come to know God better as you know me.

Reflecting theologically on human experience requires breaking into the proof circle Jesus established. It attempts to see the truth that needs no other warrant, that can have no other warrant because it is truth itself. This may feel like an unfamiliar, confusing, and even illogical way to proceed, but every other way remains in the darkness.

Like Nicodemus, theological reflectors initially approach experience in the dark, seeking the light of the one who came down from heaven (3:13), who has been lifted up in our midst like the serpent of Moses (3:14-15), who has been sent into the world by God's love, not to condemn it but to save it (3:16-17).

Like Nicodemus (and "the Jews" who disputed with Jesus), theological reflectors can see the signs that accompany experience, but they have a hard time grasping their meaning if they are not willing to think imaginatively. They may be too concerned about defining terms. They may ask questions about causal connections rather than about creative consequences, and they may seek explanations that satisfy the facts rather than interpretations that stimulate the spirit.

This type of thinking is appropriate in an academic enterprise, and it establishes the conceptual strength of a scholarly undertaking. Yet it leaves a person unprepared to meet the challenge of learning from experience or entering the persuasion of the proof circle. Lack of imagination becomes an obstacle to seeing the divine presence when a person is unwilling to let loose the full creative power of thinking and feels obliged to make sense of things only in terms of formal, logical, authoritative, or scientific knowledge. This limitation is frightening. "If you do not believe when I tell you about earthly things, how are you to believe when I tell you about those of heaven?" (3:12). Theological reflection is concerned about both and sees the imagination as a key way to bring them together.

The Last Supper Discourse

When it came to lacking imagination, Jesus' disciples excelled. This is especially evident during the first part of the last supper discourse which John presents in chapter fourteen. The whole scene is loosely patterned on the questions and answers which accompany the traditional seder meal. The disciples' interventions are designed to lead into a summary of Jesus' teaching. As preserved in the Gospel, they are not verbatim accounts. Nonetheless, they illustrate various ways the lack of imagination can pose an obstacle for theological reflection.

Jesus began his discourse by describing the many dwelling places in his Father's house and how he was going away to prepare them for the disciples before he would come back to take them with him. His description must have elicited blank stares because he added, almost rhetorically, "You know the way that leads where I go" (14:4).

This is what his whole ministry had been about; this is what he invited his disciples to share with him; this is what had led up to this night. Surely he expected their intimate experience with him to fill in the details of his imagery. Thomas, for one, was stumped by an inconsistency. "Lord, we do not know where you are going. How can we know the way?" (14:5). Thomas was practical; he dealt with what he could know in light of what he already knew. It was Thomas who concluded that they would all die with Jesus if they went back with him to pay their respects to the deceased Lazarus (11:16), and it was Thomas who would insist on touching Jesus to verify that the man he had known was now raised from the dead as the other disciples reported (20:24-29). This situation was no different.

Jesus often slipped away by himself and left the disciples to find him (as in 6:16-20). If he was planning to leave dinner early and prepare a place for them to spend the night but not tell them where, how could they know which road to take? It made sense, but not at the level Jesus was speaking. "I am the way, and the truth, and the life" (14:6). Jesus was speaking of relationships, not itineraries. He was drawing the disciples' attention to his union with the Father, which he wanted them to share through their union with him.

The theological side of reflection can be blocked by the kind of practical realism which Thomas exhibited. Instead of catching the larger spiritual meaning of a comment, an image, or a reference, theological reflectors can zero in on the logical consistency, the connection of means and ends, the practical possibility of a certain idea. This way of thinking may be very useful for pragmatic purposes ("doing" the ministry), but it often misses the theological significance of a moment and with it the divine presence being revealed.

"If you really knew me, you would know my Father also. From this point on, you know him; you have seen him" (14:7). Philip could not resist. "Lord, show us the Father and that will be enough for us" (14:8). Philip was an enthusiast; he jumped into a new situation before thinking through its implications. It was Philip who accepted Jesus' shortest invitation, "Follow me," and then shared his excitement with the cynical Nathanael, the last person we would expect to get enthusiastic about anything (2:43-46). Before he fed the multitude, Jesus asked Philip where they could buy bread, perhaps relying on his spontaneity to come up with the solution Jesus intended to carry out (6:5-7).

In this scene Philip was struck by a wonderful, new prospect: he could actually see God. He couldn't wait; he didn't need to "know" God too or understand how Jesus could make this possible. Just a glimpse was enough. In his enthusiasm he missed the main point and disappointed his Lord. "Philip, after I have been with you all this time, you still do not know me? . . . How can you say, 'Show us the Father'? Do you not believe that I am in the Father and the Father is in me?" (14:9-10)

The reflection side of theological reflection can be in-hibited by the kind of enthusiasm Philip exhibited. Instead of letting the full meaning of an experience emerge and build its own well-grounded excitement, theological reflec-tors can overreact to the first impulse of a new suggestion. The remedy is not a dispassionate approach to theological reflection, but an enthusiasm which remains imbedded in the reflection process as a whole.

Channeling Philip's enthusiasm, Jesus reiterated his union with the Father and his intention to lead the disciples into it, although it would require his going away for a time. This explanation was tailor-made for a more subtle inquiry into the nuances of the message. Judas (not Iscariot) moved in. "Lord, why is it that you will reveal yourself to us and not to the world?" (14:22).

We don't know much about this Judas. His name is included in Luke's list of the Twelve, but there is no mention of him by Matthew or Mark. (Perhaps his presence indicates that more than the Twelve attended Jesus' last supper. His question certainly reflects a concern of the Johannine community, which felt specially enlightened without being as esoteric as some gnostic sects). Judas's question reveals a systematic mind looking for connections between this specific event and a larger context of meaning — one of the goals of theological reflection.

Jesus responded in kind, suggesting two ways that "the world" can share what he has revealed to his friends. "Anyone who loves me will be true to my word and my Father will love him; and we will come to him and make our dwelling place with him" (14:23). Love is the revealing gift, and everyone is capable of loving and being loved. But there's more.

"The Paraclete, the Holy Spirit, whom the Father will send in my name, will instruct you in everything and remind you of all that I told you" (14:26). Jesus will not remain a mere memory, his message a series of formulas to be recited. The connections between his tiny band of disciples and the human race; between the slim strip of land on the shore of the Mediterranean and the whole world; between his few years of public service and the destiny of history are not to be worked out in mental schemas. They will be lived out in the power of a new Spirit, even if Jesus is not visibly present with them.

Theological reflection can be bogged down in the desire to see the largest generalizable effect from each particular event. On the other hand, the ability to see the macrocosm in the microcosm is a gift, an exercise of imagination which avoids fantasy and glimpses reality in its wholeness. It is a gift given by the Spirit, and cultivated by theological reflection.

SELF-PROTECTION

The starting point of theological reflection is usually a particular experience. The goal is to find in that experience signs of the divine presence which will lead to an encounter with God. The assumption is that theological reflectors come to the experience with an open mind, willing to learn from it and let themselves be challenged by it. But sometimes the opposite is the case. Reflectors can feel threatened and want to protect themselves against the implications of an experience even when they appear to be sincerely looking for the divine presence. In this case the experience interprets the reflectors rather than the other way around, and their pretense becomes an obstacle to theological reflection, as the following stories illustrate.

The Adulteress

The story of the woman caught in adultery is inserted into the disputes between Jesus and "the Jews" during the Feast of Booths (7:1–8:59). It is not clear where it really belongs or whether it was originally part of John's Gospel. As a lesson for theological reflection, however, it is worth examining.

After spending the night on the Mount of Olives, Jesus returned to the temple area and resumed teaching. He was interrupted by the scribes and Pharisees, who brought before him a woman caught in adultery. Their disregard for her is poignantly described: "They made her stand there in front of everyone" (8:3). They cared nothing for the woman; their purpose was to trap Jesus in a dilemma.

"In the law," they recited, "Moses ordered such women to be stoned. What do you have to say about the case?" They did not even treat her as a woman; she was a case. If

Jesus sided with the letter of the law, he would seem to retract his gospel of mercy, forgiveness, and freedom. If he advocated a breach of the law, he would contradict his own claim to be fulfilling what Moses set down. The trap was set; the dilemma was in place. How would Jesus respond?

He began to doodle. At least, that's one interpretation of the sentence, "Jesus bent down and started tracing on the ground with his finger" (8:6). He knew that the woman and her situation were being exploited for theological triumph, not for theological reflection. He wouldn't play along.

When experience is misused in a theological reflection group, it is rarely so contrived or manipulative as this and people are not exposed so cruelly. However, it can happen that some reflectors are so intent on proving their point or confronting the opinions of peers that they can manipulate an experience for this purpose rather than to discover where God may be found and how they should respond.

The proponents were persistent; they kept asking Jesus for an opinion. Once committed, they could not let go of their strategy. Rather than be controlled by their scheme and drawn into their abuse of the woman, Jesus put the situation in its proper theological context, the one they ostensibly were concerned about: sin.

"Let the man among you who has no sin be the first to cast a stone at her" (8:7). Where did this response come from and what did it mean? Jesus' antagonists did not ask an abstract question about a legal interpretation. They presented him with a real person in a real situation. And Jesus identified with her. He no doubt saw in her and in the way she was being treated the terrible effects of sin. He knew what a grip it had on people, as John's Gospel earlier noted, "He needed no one to give him testimony about human nature. He was well aware of what was in man's heart" (2:25). Perhaps in her he caught a glimpse of his own eventual degradation at the hands of these same officials.

Out of this deep, compassionate bond he responded to their question as if to say: "Sin is the human disordering of God's creation. Only God can finally put it right. If you think you're on God's level (as they accused him of claiming for himself), then do what you think God would do." He went back to doodling, not to make light of the situation but to show his disregard for their misuse of it and to leave the dilemma with them.

When someone exploits a situation in theological reflection, it is incumbent on the group to restore the focus. This is rarely done by directly confronting the motives of the person who led the discussion astray or responding to the misleading question/comment. It is more successful to pick up what the person has said and use it to restate the central question: where is God in this experience? The reflectors must then decide which path to follow.

"Then the audience drifted away one by one, beginning with the elders" (8:9). It is interesting that the scribes and Pharisees are not named as the ones who begin to leave but "the audience," presumably those whom Jesus had been teaching, who were more in touch with God's ways than their learned leaders. It is also noteworthy that the elders left first, as if their longer experience with life and sin, with judgment and punishment, enabled them to hear the wisdom of Jesus' answer. In any event the redirection which Jesus gave to the incident brought him face to face with the woman and the reality she represented.

"Woman, where did they all disappear to? Has no one condemned you?" "No one, sir," she answered. "Nor do I condemn you" (8:10-11). In his view this situation never was about condemnation; it was about life and recognizing God's presence in the midst of it. Consequently, "You may go. But from now on avoid this sin."

Jesus did not let the majority opinion of the crowd determine his view, nor did he disregard the gravity of her sin. He let the situation reveal what was at stake, for the woman and for God. He named what he saw and he drew the appropriate conclusion. This is the goal of theological reflection. It is difficult enough to achieve when everyone is working together; it faces a major obstacle when someone misuses the experience for a contrary purpose.

Anointing at Bethany

A similar incident exposing false motives is narrated in chapter twelve. The scene is heavy with death and the threat of death. At the end of chapter eleven the Sanhedrin had met to discuss how they might eliminate Jesus. Their motive, according to John's account, was self-preservation. "If we let him go on like this [he had just raised Lazarus from the dead], the whole world will believe in him. Then the Romans will come in and sweep away our sanctuary and our nation" (11:48).

The stakes were indeed high. For the Sanhedrin it came down to a choice between Jesus and their way of life. If one of the two had to go, it was clear which it would be. "From that day onward there was a plan afoot to kill him" (11:53), and "anyone who knew where he was should report it, so that they could apprehend him" (11:57).

For a while Jesus kept his distance from Jerusalem, but as Passover approached, so did he. He came to Bethany and was given a banquet. Martha was serving (as we might expect from Luke's portrayal of her). Lazarus was also at table, making the scene a striking embodiment of the messianic banquet and the resurrection of the dead which Martha had confessed to Jesus in chapter eleven. This motif continued when Mary entered the scene.

Mary, who has been traditionally depicted as a contemplative sitting at Jesus' feet while Martha handled domestic chores, was now very much a woman of action. She brought a pound of expensive perfume and used it to anoint Jesus' feet. Her act was not only public, it was intimate as she dried his feet with her hair. With the aroma filling the house, the question arose: what does this mean?

Judas Iscariot was quick to assess. "Why was not this perfume sold? It could have brought three hundred silver pieces and the money have been given to the poor" (12:5). A compelling consideration, except that Judas didn't mean it. As the Gospel narrator notes, "He did not say this out of concern for the poor, but because he was a thief." He may have had other motives as well.

Perhaps he was getting nervous about his impending role in handing Jesus over to the authorities (12:4). Whatever his motives for doing this, they must have been confronted by Mary's lavish display of affection. Her perfume was ten times more expensive than his payment would be. The more he saw what Jesus meant to Mary (and others), the harder it would be to carry out his deed, to block his second thoughts. In this case the event exposed Judas to himself.

Theological reflection can have a similar impact. The meaning of an experience can confront a person's prior convictions or motives and suggest that a change is in order, sometimes a rather profound change. When a person reacts by immediately attacking the experience and dismissing its overt value for another apparently higher value, it is a sign that the experience has struck home. In order to help the person deal with this inner turmoil, it is important to keep the focus on the real meaning of the experience. Jesus does this rather abruptly.

"Leave her alone." Jesus did not let Judas take out his personal discomfort by attacking Mary any more than he would let the scribes and Pharisees trap him by using the woman caught in adultery. Instead Jesus drew attention to the meaning of her act, a meaning which embraced Judas's reaction as well. "Let her keep it against the day they prepare me for burial" (12:7). Both Mary and Judas were players in the drama of Jesus' death. Mary was unaware of it even though her anointing dramatized it. Judas was aware of it even though his pretense tried to hide it. Jesus seemed willing to let the experience stand as it was and not be misused. "The poor you always have with you, but me you will not always have" (12:8).

Theological reflection has access to a particular experience for only a short time. In that time the experience can be very revealing, not only of the divine presence but of the reflectors as well. Sometimes what is revealed is not comfortable, but the task of theological reflection is to remain focused on the meaning of the experience and to let its truth emerge, whatever the implications. This is a lesson Pilate was unwilling to learn.

Dialogue with Pilate

As John narrates it, Jesus' meeting with Pilate began at daybreak. The darkness which has pervaded the Gospel's story was beginning to clear as events headed toward their climax. Jesus had spent the night being interrogated by the high priesthood of Israel, represented by Annas and Caiaphas (18:13 and 19:24). The scene now shifts from religious authority to secular authority, represented by Pilate.

Pilate seemed eager to dispatch this religious squabble as quickly as possible. "What accusation do you bring against this man?" (18:29). Jesus' accusers reassured him. "If he were not a criminal, we would certainly not have handed him over to you" (18:30). Pilate was not convinced this warranted his attention. "Why do you not take him and pass judgment on him according to your law?" Jesus' accusers pressed the gravity of the case. He had committed a capital crime and "we may not put anyone to death." These were Rome's regulations; "the Jews" were only being dutiful subjects.

Pilate could not escape. He had to confront this issue. In doing so, he revealed who he was and what his values were. Sometimes an issue in theological reflection has the same impact. The reflectors cannot avoid it, and their response to it reveals more of themselves than they intend.

Pilate apparently dealt with things straight on. He went to Jesus and asked directly, "Are you the King of the Jews?" (18:33). This accusation had not been mentioned in the session with Pilate, but it permeates the Gospel and was obviously the civil charge which was brought against Jesus. At face value it implied a treasonous position, something Pilate would have to resolve as the representative of Rome's emperor. All Jesus had to do was deny it (as he had avoided the title and its implications throughout his ministry), and the trial would be over. Instead he probed Pilate.

"Are you saying this on your own, or have others been telling you about me?" (18:34). Jesus wanted to know if Pilate's question was coming from his own experience or from the reports of others. In other words, was he personally involved in this case or just doing his duty.

The same question arises in theological reflection.

Often it is prompted by the standard, almost clichéd, question, "How are you feeling about this?" The intent of the question is to determine if the reflectors are expressing their own experience or merely repeating someone else's opinion, fulfilling a requirement, going through the motions. Like many theological reflectors, Pilate did not like the question.

"I am no Jew! It is your own people and the chief priests who have handed you over to me" (18:35). Not only was Pilate not personally involved, he didn't want to be involved. He just wanted to get through this exercise (like many a theological reflector who would rather discuss theological principles than share personal feelings). "What have you done?"

Jesus accepted Pilate's preference and perspective but kept him focused on experience. "My kingdom does not belong to this world. If my kingdom were of this world, my subjects would be fighting to save me from being handed over to the Jews" (18:36). In other words, look for yourself. If I were the kind of king you suppose, the kind my accusers want you to see, my followers would be disrupting these proceedings and fighting to rescue me. Do you see that happening? My kingship is no threat to your rule.

Jesus tried to open Pilate to the deeper significance of what was going on, to offer a different interpretation. Yet Pilate already knew what kind of answer he was looking for. "So, then, you are a king?" It didn't matter what kind of king. Nuances and conceptual refinements were not his concern. He dealt with facts, answers, decisions.

Sometimes those threatened by the direction of a theological reflection protect themselves by dismissing careful thinking as so much distraction, preferring to deal with the obvious, the concrete, the controllable. They may even misconstrue what another says when it hits too close to home.

"It is you who say I am a king" (18:37). Don't put words in my mouth or draw conclusions which don't follow from what I said. Listen better, enter the experience, let it guide you. "The reason I was born, the reason why I came into the world, is to testify to the truth. Anyone committed to the truth hears my voice" (18:37).

This is the ultimate challenge of theological reflection — the truth of a concrete event. There are many obstacles to recognizing and affirming the truth, but the unwillingness to be exposed as a seeker of divine truth is one of the most stubborn. Pilate dismissed the challenge by belittling it. "Truth! What does that mean?" (18:38). He would handle the situation his way rather than the ambiguous, uncomfortable way of Jesus (and of theological reflection).

First, he confronted "the Jews" with his impression. "Speaking for myself [finally] I find no case against this man" (18:38). Then he offered a practical alternative which would let everyone save face. Who is worse, this solitary man with no supporters or the insurrectionist, Barabbas, whose guerilla activities have already brought reprisals on Jerusalem — the very thing the Sanhedrin feared (11:48)? "The Jews" could take Jesus and praise themselves for protecting their people's welfare. Pilate, on the other hand, could uphold the custom of releasing an agitator to the Jews, thus enhancing his status with the people. Case closed.

But the crowd shouted, "We want Barabbas, not this one!" (18:39-40). Pilate must have been shocked. They would take the greater risk by releasing Barabbas? Why did they hate this Jesus so much? Why did they want his blood? Rather than pursue the question, Pilate stayed true to his pragmatic course. If they wanted blood, he would give it to them. He had Jesus scourged, thus beginning the crucifixion process and expecting that it would end right there.

The sight of a scourged and humiliated Jesus seemed to whet the crowd's appetite rather than satisfy it. "Look at the man!" he implored. "Crucify him!" they insisted. Pilate was losing his interest in this standoff. "Take him and crucify him yourselves." And lest there be any doubt about his position, "I find no case against him" (19:6). Pilate revealed himself under the pressure of the situation. He was not guided by the strength of his convictions; he was not really interested in the truth (or justice) of the case. He only wanted to get it out of the way, even if he had to bend the rules to let "the Jews" carry out their execution.

Theological reflectors are rarely so crass in dismissing the theological challenges of a situation or deciding on a course of action. But something of every reflector is indeed revealed by the reflection process. When it becomes uncomfortable or unclear, a reflector can look for an easy escape route by trivializing the situation or dismissing its theological claims. The other reflectors should not let this happen, just as "the Jews" did not let Pilate shift his responsibility to them.

"We have our law and according to that law he must die because he made himself God's Son." This was their real aggravation with Jesus. It was the reason that first prompted thoughts of putting him to death. "The Jews" seemed to admit that they used the "King of the Jews" accusation to get Pilate's attention, but now they wanted him to know how serious they were. The situation made them more honest. It had its effect on Pilate too.

"When Pilate heard this kind of talk, he was more afraid than ever" (19:8). Underneath his officious and commanding presence, Pilate was frightened — frightened that the crowd could get out of hand and endanger him physically; frightened that if he botched this trial, his reputation with Rome would be weakened. Pilate was frightened, in short, for himself. He tried to regroup, look for solid ground where he could reestablish his authority. He went back to Jesus, the prisoner with no supporters, and tried to start over.

"Where do you come from?" (19:9). Jesus had heard this question repeatedly from those who tried to discredit his message by discrediting his authority to proclaim it. Pilate was testy: "Do you refuse to speak to me? Do you not know that I have the power to release you and the power to crucify you?" (19:10). Unable to persuade, Pilate resorted to threats. Even so, Jesus saw an opening in Pilate's desperation and offered him another chance to share the meaning of this event.

"You would have no power over me whatever unless it were given you from above." For Jesus, every moment was a revelation of God's presence and action; each person was a player in God's drama: "That is why he who handed me over to you is guilty of the greater sin" (19:11). It's hard to tell what Pilate made of this. Perhaps he heard Jesus reminding him of his official delegation and his duty to satisfy the "higher authorities" in Rome; perhaps he felt that he and Jesus were finally communicating, were finally dealing with practical matters. Whatever his understanding, the Gospel says that "after this, Pilate was eager to release him" (19:12).

But Pilate's momentary desire was no match for his need to survive. Confronted again by "the Jews" and *their* reminder that he would be no friend of Caesar's if he released Jesus, he went through the motions of adjudication, but "in the end, Pilate handed Jesus over to be crucified" (19:16). Unable to respond to the truth of the situation as it emerged, Pilate took refuge in the security of his role and thereby exposed his true self.

Theological reflection can pose the same challenge. As reflectors enter in and analyze a person's experience, they can expose shortcomings in thinking, behavior, and skill that the person would rather avoid. Like Pilate, a person can hold on to a previous self-image and try to make the experience fit it or face the new perspective which reflection offers and change in response to it. Such change is not easy, but the alternative is to become more self-protective, more authoritarian, and often more angry, as Pilate showed.

When he issued the crime for which Jesus was crucified, he used the wording of "the Jews" who instigated the trial, shoving the episode back in their faces: "Jesus the Nazarene, the King of the Jews." The chief priests objected, perhaps sensing that Pilate was still vulnerable to their pressure. They wanted him to say, "This man claimed to be King of the Jews." Pilate summoned his damaged ego and firmly asserted, "What I have written, I have written" (19:22). Just as resolutely, he refused to change who he was, even when confronted with truth itself.

SUMMARY

Recognizing the divine presence is impeded by an unwillingness to be led by experience and to learn from it. John's Gospel describes the obstacles to theological reflection in the following ways.

1. Reliance on external authority can prevent a person from seeing the authority inherent in an experience.

2. Reliance on external authority can prevent a person from seeing the positive effects of an unusual action which doesn't fit what is considered acceptable.

3. Theological reflectors can expect to face opposition from those who rely on external authority.

4. Reliance on external authority inclines a person to judge events by appearances rather than by their inner meaning and to presume a greater grasp of the truth than is possible.

5. Lack of imagination can prevent a person from recognizing the spiritual meaning of an experience, especially if it is conveyed through symbols, metaphors, and analogies.

6. Lack of imagination limits theological reflection to the definition of terms and criteria of logical thought.

7. Imagination can be impeded by pragmatic concerns, an impulsive enthusiasm, or a preoccupation with "generalizable" conclusions.

8. A person's refusal to share feelings and opinions honestly is an obstacle to theological reflection.

9. A person can exploit an experience to prove a point or manipulate a peer.

10. A person can profess false motives during a theological reflection in order to look good, gain acceptance, or save face.

11. A person's immediate concern, such as fear of losing status or reputation, may replace higher values, such as truth and justice.

12. A person may trivialize or dismiss the theological importance of an experience to avoid being honestly exposed.

CHAPTER 4

Theological Reflection during a Ministerial Event

Theological reflection usually occurs after the fact. A student selects an event, describes it, presents it to a supervisor and/or peer group, and then reflects on it theologically. This is very useful for acquiring the skill of theological reflection, but it also has some drawbacks.

Reflecting after the fact tends to benefit the minister but not the person(s) ministered to in the original event. The opportunity for recognizing the divine presence with them in that setting is over. Of course, if the minister is reflecting on an event which is part of a continuing series (as in counseling or extended pastoral care), the insights from one encounter may be carried over to the next. Even in this case, however, reflection on a prior meeting may not be relevant to the next occasion. The minister's desire to work them in may even get in the way of recognizing the divine presence in the present event as it unfolds.

It seems valuable, then, for ministers to be able to engage in theological reflection during an encounter as well as after it. Fortunately, the skill needed to recognize the divine presence in an event while it is happening is not really different from the skill needed to gain insight into an event after it has happened. The problem is that so much happens during an event, it may be difficult to focus on the theological aspect.

John's Gospel provides a unique example of how theological reflection may occur as part of an interpersonal dialogue. The incident contains a working model of theological reflection, whether it is done during or after an event. The episode is Jesus' discussion with the Samaritan woman at the well.

JESUS AND THE SAMARITAN WOMAN

Jesus didn't intend any competition with John the Baptizer, but it arose anyway. He and his disciples were in Judean territory "and he spent some time with them there baptizing" (John 3:22). The Gospel later corrects the obvious meaning of this text (perhaps to insure that Jesus would not be seen as imitating the Baptizer) by saying parenthetically "in fact, it was not Jesus himself who baptized but his disciples" (4:2).

The problem was, John *the* Baptizer was working the same area, and some of his disciples, already in a dispute with a certain Jew about purification, were uneasy with Jesus' success. "Everyone is flocking to him," they complained (3:26). John, on the other hand, must have felt relieved. This was exactly how it was supposed to be. "He must increase while I must decrease" (3:30), a worthy maxim for theological reflectors.

Even John's impending imprisonment could not stifle

his mood. He felt like the best man at a wedding (perhaps the Gospel author was still mulling over the events at Cana, recorded in the previous chapter). "The groom's best man waits there listening for him and is overjoyed to hear his voice. That is my joy, and it is complete" (3:29) — the same sentiment Jesus would express before his own impending arrest (15:11; 17:13).

Yet this early success scared Jesus off. When he learned that the Pharisees knew his numbers were higher than John's, he headed for home. It was one thing to inherit John's popularity; it was quite another to take on the scrutiny and antagonism that accompanied it.

Jesus took a circuitous route, perhaps to confuse the Pharisees, and it landed him and his disciples right in the midst of the Samaritans. The disciples must have wondered which was worse: skirting the suspicions of the Pharisees with whom they were not yet in personal conflict or entering the territory of the Samaritans with whom they were locked in long-standing religious animosity. Jesus seemed oblivious to everything but his tired feet. He sent the disciples into the village to buy food while he sat down and waited.

Along came a woman from the village, hauling her supply of water. Perhaps it was the splash of her bucket at the bottom of the well or perhaps it was the fact that she was doing this particular daily chore that made him realize he was thirsty. No matter. What happened next is a model of theological reflection.

Setting

The setting was painfully ordinary. It was the middle of the day. Jesus was resting, tired and hungry from his journey. A woman was going about her daily chores. Nothing very special, the way much of a minister's day is spent. But John alerts the reader that this setting is not as ordinary as it appears.

Jesus stopped "near the plot of land which Jacob had given to his son Joseph. This was the site of Jacob's well" (4:5-6). It doesn't matter that the Old Testament does not mention this well or that scholars dispute the name of the town. The setting is special because the shapers of Jewish history have been here. The deeds of Jacob and Joseph linger, mingling with the daily activities which continue to fill this space. Perhaps the divine spirit which moved through them is still moving, breathing life, shaping dreams, uttering sacred words — just as the Spirit does in the settings where ministry occurs today.

Consider a hospital. What heroic deeds and inspiring stories have come from the patients' rooms, the operating rooms, the waiting rooms, the labs and hallways? How many life-and-death decisions have been made here? How many times has God been invoked in prayer and sacrament to share the uncertainty and fear and struggle of illness? How many saints have left the earth from this very place? And how many have returned to their families and friends, their livelihoods and neighborhoods, healed and confirmed in their trust of God?

No setting is so ordinary that it lacks the presence of God. The first task of a theologically alert minister, therefore, is to pay attention to the setting as John did; to have an eye for the depth of the well, a feel for the thickness of the space, a taste for the refreshment hidden within the water. Then the minister can enter the experience.

Entry

"Give me a drink," Jesus said. This request probably does not surprise us; he was thirsty and she had water. But the woman knew her history. "You are a Jew. How can you ask me, a Samaritan and a woman, for a drink?" Her resistance was consistent with deep cultural feelings, as John informs those unacquainted with the customs of that time. "Recall that Jews have nothing to do with Samaritans" (4:9), not to mention men with women in public. Jesus was clearly stepping out of line, entering where he didn't belong, and this woman wanted to put him in his place.

A minister visiting patients in a hospital or parishioners can sometimes get the same reaction. Asking an innocuous, commonplace, and perfectly friendly question like, "How are you feeling today?" can elicit a response like, "What do you mean, how do I feel? I'm full of tubes and needles, and the doctor thinks I may have cancer. How do you think I feel?"

Such a comment, like the bite of the Samaritan woman's retort, can easily make a minister feel defensive or intimidated. Jesus seemed to welcome it, but his response must be interpreted carefully as a model of theological re-flection. "If only you recognized God's gift, and who it is that is asking you for a drink, you would have asked him instead, and he would have given you living water" (4:10).

This passage does not permit a minister to enter another person's space thinking "I am God's gift to this person and I possess exactly what this person needs (and better ask for)." But it does encourage a minister to enter another person's space with confidence, sure of God's pres-ence no matter how ordinary the setting or distressed the person. This confidence is verified by the situation as it unfolds, and the key to the situation is the other person.

Jesus recognized this by starting with the woman's concern and using it to look with her more deeply into her experience. She could only see a Jew asking her for water in violation of custom. Jesus suggested that if she would look at the same situation with an eye for God's gift, she might see him differently, relate to him differently, and thereby discover a different source of water for herself. The woman was attentive but skeptical.

"You do not have a bucket and this well is deep. Where do you expect to get this flowing water?" (4:11). She could not yet see past the standing water at the bottom of the well, but Jesus had prodded her to envision the fresh coolness of a bubbling spring. Once under way, her imagination kept running. "Maybe this man knows of a secret spring or a hidden depth where the water is better. But how could he know that?"

"Surely you do not pretend to be greater than our ancestor Jacob, who gave us this well and drank from it with his sons and his flocks?" (4:12). Jesus sensed that she was tapping into their common history, into the reservoir of people and deeds that linked them at a deep level.

"Everyone who drinks this water will be thirsty again. But whoever drinks the water I give will never be thirsty. No, the water I give shall become a fountain within, leaping up to provide eternal life" (4:13-14). Jesus did not abandon or discount the woman's concern with the well water she had to carry every day; instead he used it to offer her a new kind of water — better even than spring water!— a fountain, a constant, effervescent surge of refreshment.

The woman was open — "Give me this water" — but for her own reasons, "so that I shall not grow thirsty and have to keep coming here to draw water" (4:15). Jesus arrived at the second stage of theological reflection. He opened a new dimension in the woman's experience. He did not impose his own religious message or replace her agenda with his. He entered her situation, used her concerns and terms, and suggested a deeper meaning than the woman was aware of when they began speaking.

At this point theological reflection can lead to the kind of personal revelation discussed at the end of the last chapter. Jesus approached this moment in an unexpected way. "Go, call your husband and then come back here" (4:16). This seems like an abrupt departure from their conversation about thirst and wells and fountains. The woman responded tersely: "I have no husband" (4:17).

In John Jesus is depicted as having complete knowledge and mastery of every situation. The present scene is no exception. "You are right in saying you have no husband. The fact is, you have had five, and the man you are living with now is not your husband" (4:17-18).

On the surface this comment seems to veer off into personal details that are irrelevant to the theological point which was emerging. This is always a temptation in theological reflection, especially if the reflectors are fascinated by the psychological or behavioral aspects of the people in the situation. Was Jesus getting distracted (after all, he was still thirsty and hadn't eaten) or is there a lesson here for theological reflection?

The lesson might be this. Theological reflectors enter people's experience and elicit their personal beliefs and understandings. To participate it is not necessary to have a particular level of formal, theological knowledge or be in a church-approved program of ministry. One need not meet a particular standard of holiness or moral conduct to have insights into the divine presence. This is what Jesus seemed to say to the woman, acknowledging but subordinating her marital situation just as he acknowledged but subordinated the adultery of the woman in chapter eight.

In the same vein, mere information about someone's personal life doesn't have much to do with theological reflection. Theological reflection is not interested in exposing the private details of people to one another; it is interested in revealing God to people through one another. What is needed is honesty, respect, and a willingness to share one's views, relying on their intrinsic value, not on external authority or status (as analyzed in chapter three).

The woman may have caught the point Jesus was making, or she may have wanted to avoid any further discussion of her personal life. In either case she moved into the next phase of theological reflection by turning the conversation back on Jesus in a way familiar to every minister.

Theological Learning

"Sir, I can see you are a prophet" (4:19). There was a touch of flattery in this statement, not unlike a person acknowledging to a minister, "I can see you really know your Bible." If her praise was calculated to keep him at a distance from her personal life, it also exploited his competence (a tactic frequently used on ministers when they move too close for comfort). She asked him *the* religious question that had divided Jews and Samaritans for generations.

"Our ancestors worshiped on this mountain, but you people claim that Jerusalem is the place where people ought to worship God" (4:20). Which is it, she seemed to imply. Jesus accepted her inquiry, letting it lead him (and her) into a larger framework.

"Believe me, woman, an hour is coming when you will worship the Father neither on this mountain nor in Jerusalem" (4:21). Jesus restated her question, lifting it out of the confinement of a theological stalemate and placing it in the context of its true meaning — worship of the Father. This is the goal of theological reflection: to take the questions which arise in ordinary conversation and follow them, not into the nuances of diverse schools of thought, but into the nucleus of belief from which they came.

This is not easy. It is often unclear what the questions mean, how they should be phrased, where they come from or where they lead. Theological reflection does not promise answers ahead of time; it only offers a process for seeking, and sometimes discovering.

In his search with the Samaritan woman Jesus used his own preferred language — worship of "the Father" — and he also gave his opinion on the question she asked: "You people worship what you do not understand, while we understand what we worship; after all, salvation is from the Jews" (4:22). But he was more interested in getting at the meaning behind the question, the nature of true worship.

"Yet an hour is coming, and is already here, when authentic worshipers will worship the Father in spirit and truth. Indeed it is just such worshipers the Father seeks. God is Spirit and those who worship God must worship in Spirit and truth" (4:23-24). These verses rush from each other filling the space just opened for theological learning. Characteristic Johannine terms (the hour, already here, the Father, Spirit and truth) channel the message to its conclusion.

The Samaritan woman joined in with her own contribution: "I know there is a Messiah coming. When he comes, he will tell us everything" (4:25). On this, Jews and Samaritans could agree. Her declaration allowed Jesus to disclose, in typical Johannine fashion, "I who speak to you am he" (4:26). Needless to say, the goal of theological reflection is not to serve the minister's messianic aspirations but to discover the presence of the Messiah in the midst of everyday circumstances. Now is the hour; this is the occasion; here is the Lord. Not every theological reflection will lead to such a deep recognition of the saving presence of God, but every theological reflection should follow the same pattern in seeking it.

Enactment

When theological reflection works, it prompts the participants to put into practice what they have discovered or learned. John narrates this dramatically. Just at the theological climax of the conversation between Jesus and the woman, the disciples return. Like the Samaritan woman herself, the disciples "were surprised that Jesus was speaking with a woman" (4:27), but they resisted asking him about it. Perhaps they'd already learned not to question his unconventional behavior unless they wanted to become a foil for his next teaching.

The woman may have been caught off guard by their return or she may have been unable to restrain her enthusiasm any longer. "The woman then left her water jar and went off into the town" (4:28). Leaving her water jar symbolizes the change she experienced. She was no longer an anonymous water carrier in an obscure Samaritan village. She had become a herald to her townspeople, preparing the way of the Lord (like that other water figure, John, who opened this story). "Come and see someone who told me everything I did! Could this not be the Messiah?" (4:29).

The woman wasted little time with "ice breakers" or environmental conditioning. She spoke from her own experience (not learned formulas) and with her own wonder (not practiced ministerial style). She was assertive, insistent, authentic, and compelling. "At that they set out from the town to meet him" (4:30).

Jesus was changed too. His disciples were urging him, "Rabbi, eat something" (4:31), but the hunger he had initially felt when he sent them into the village had been satisfied. "I have food to eat of which you do not know" (4:32). Like the Samaritan woman, the disciples took him literally. "Do you suppose that someone has brought him something to eat?" their irritation rising at the thought that the trip they just made into unfriendly quarters was wasted.

But Jesus was pondering the effect of his conversation with the woman. What did it tell him about the shape of his work? It was still early in his ministry, the formative period. Was this type of conversation what his Father wanted of him rather than premature interventions such as at the wedding celebration in Cana (2:1-11) or public confrontations like the cleansing of the temple (2:13-22) or clandestine meetings with Jewish leaders like Nicodemus (3:1-21)? How did they all fit together? These are a minister's questions. They are the questions which theological reflection can prompt, and sometimes answer.

"Doing the will of him who sent me and bringing his work to completion is my food" (4:34). Jesus must have been feeling satisfied with his conversation with the woman; he must have longed for fifteen minutes like that with every person he met. If he could do that, he would never have to eat, the experience would be so exhilarating, so energizing, so fulfilling. But the disciples were standing around him, lunch in their hands and bewilderment on their faces.

> Do you not have a saying: "Four months more and it will be harvest!"? Listen to what I say: Open your eyes

and see! The fields are shining for harvest! The reaper already collects his wages and gathers a yield for eternal life, that sower and reaper may rejoice together. Here we have the saying verified: "One man sows; another reaps." I sent you to reap what you had not worked for. Others have done the labor, and you have come into their gain" (4:35-38).

The food and hunger motif no doubt suggested this saying and the analogy of the harvest to the author of the Gospel, if not to Jesus. Theological reflection also works like this: a word or gesture gives rise to an image or metaphor which triggers an analogy which leads back to a saying which sets a course of action. It is a creative, often spontaneous enterprise, alert to what's happening now: "open your eyes and see!"

Theological reflection is not primarily a solitary undertaking. It feeds off the interaction and contributions of many people: "one sows; another reaps." And it embraces and rewards all who participate: "sower and reaper rejoice together." The process continues as those who reflect draw upon the wisdom of the past while handing on their own insights for the future: "others have done the labor and you have come into their gain."

This stretches the harvest reference beyond its original function in John — in order to supply the eucharistic counterpart to the baptismal theme in Jesus' conversation with the woman and to remind the second generation Christians that they are the beneficiaries of the work of their predecessors. The last point is especially pertinent to theological reflection and is heightened by the way John ends this story.

At first "many Samaritans from that town believed in him on the strength of the woman's word of testimony"

(4:39). She had done for them what Jesus had done for her. Her ministry was effective, so much so that "they begged him to stay with them awhile. So he stayed there two days" (4:40). She turned them over to Jesus and in doing so she terminated their dependency on her. "No longer does our faith depend on your story. We have heard for ourselves, and we know that this really is the Savior of the world" (4:42).

This is the ultimate criterion of theological reflection: that people do not remain dependent on a minister or expert or convener or reflection guide to tell them where the Lord is in their own experience. Rather people become interdependent, discovering with one another where the Lord is by entering their ordinary situations together, helping to probe the deeper meaning of those situations, and enacting the results.

SUMMARY

The conversation of Jesus with the Samaritan woman is an example of theological reflection during a ministerial encounter. The chief lessons to be derived are these.

1. Theological reflection can begin in the most ordinary, familiar circumstances.

2. Theological significance is often discovered by making associations with the facts of the situation: thirst and water suggest baptism and eternal life; hunger and food suggest eucharist and mission.

3. Theological reflection requires entering into a person's situation, even if it means meeting some resistance.

4. A person's theological insights are not predetermined by academic, professional, personal, or even moral status.

5. Every theological question can open a larger, more inclusive, and revealing vision.

6. A clear criterion of the success of theological reflection is the desire of reflectors to act on what they have recognized.

7. The goal of theological reflection is for each reflector to recognize the divine presence in their own experience, with the help of others but not dependence on them.

CHAPTER 5

Theological Reflection in a Group

Theological reflection works best when it is done in a group. Group discussion can uncover aspects of an experience which an individual might overlook. This enhances the potential for learning from the experience. In addition, members of a group can keep one another honest by raising the critical questions which an individual might privately avoid.

From a Christian and ministerial point of view, there are additional values in group reflection. Christianity is primarily a communal experience; it is a shared life and comes to fullest expression in the exchanges which create community — whether it is the community of two or three, a family, a seminar, a staff, or a congregation. Theological reflection groups are a prime example of this and provide one more opportunity to experience Christian community.

Correspondingly, a great deal of the Christian ministry occurs within groups. Learning how to function in a group and how a group functions are valuable lessons for the Christian minister, and theological reflection groups are an excellent setting in which this learning can occur. However, there are some drawbacks to a group discussion.

Individuals do not always agree, and their differences can lead to conflict which distracts from the primary goal of theological reflection. Some individuals also have hidden or personal items which they insert into a discussion, forcing the group to deal with their agenda rather than what the experience can teach. Group discussion is often untidy, raising issues which are not resolved, opening lines of thought which are not fully pursued, and generating feelings which are not always dealt with.

Theological reflection embraces both the potential and the drawbacks of group reflection. What this means and how it may be dealt with can be seen in chapter nine of John's Gospel.

CURE OF THE BLIND MAN

Event

Chapter nine begins casually: "As he walked along, he saw a man who had been blind from birth" (9:1). The author gives no indication of the time or place, but the Johannine irony is evident: Jesus sees a man who can't see anything, and never has. Perhaps he paused to gaze at the man, perhaps he gave some indication that this scene was significant. His disciples, alert to his clues, jumped in.

"'Rabbi, was it his sin or that of his parents that caused him to be born blind?'" (9:2). They had acquired the student's instinct for posing questions to show they were thinking theologically. They could take a specific case and immediately raise theological questions, initiating an informed and engaging discussion. They could just as well have been sitting around a seminar table in a seminary classroom, looking to the teacher after making their point to see how impressed he was.

"'Neither,' answered Jesus" (9:3). The disciples' minds went searching. Was there an opinion they had overlooked? Had they misstated the question? Was Jesus paying attention? "'It was no sin, either of this man or of his parents. Rather, it was to let God's works show forth in him'" (9:3).

Typically Jesus took the starting point given to him (this time by his disciples) and used it to broaden the perspective and lead to action — precisely the goal of theological reflection. In this case sin was a short-range explanation. Like some theological assessments it analyzed a situation without improving it. The criterion Jesus invoked is the standard for theological reflection (and ultimately all theologizing): to let God's works show forth in the situation (a reference he used in his disputes with "the Jews," noted earlier). He drove home this point with some urgency. "'We must do the deeds of him who sent me while it is day. The night comes on when no one can work. While I am in the world I am the light of the world'" (9:4-5).

The familiar Johannine interplay between light and darkness, day and night, as well as the imminence of the hour of salvation enrich this saying. So too does the condition of the blind man. Perhaps that's what Jesus saw in him, a symbol of the darkness that traps so many and prevents them from letting God's works show forth in them. In that sense sin *is* "at work" here, not as a causal explanation for this man's handicap, but as a competing force, resisting God's work to enlighten the world and postpone nightfall.

In any event, Jesus wasted no time putting his reflection into practice. In contrast to the heady arguments with the Pharisees and "the Jews" which filled most of chapter eight, Jesus indulged in physical, tactile, almost coarse behavior. "With that Jesus spat on the ground, made mud with his saliva, and smeared the man's eyes with the mud. Then he told him, 'Go, wash in the pool of Siloam'" (9:6-7).

The man must have wondered what was going on. He had not been privy to the discussion between Jesus and the disciples, but here he was at the center of that discussion's action. There is a caution here for theological reflection. Key people, like a hospital patient, a grieving parishioner, a homeless person, whose experience initiates the reflection, can be left out of the discussion. They may be the recipients of whatever action the reflection leads to, but they do not necessarily contribute to the reflection which leads to that action. In such a case the theological reflection is one-sided, and the group doing it is too narrow.

Like most of the "insignificant" people in the Gospel who heard Jesus' word, this man reacted immediately — and with marvelous effect. "So the man went off and washed, and came back able to see" (9:7). Theological reflection does not pretend to have such direct and positive power, but it does aim at action which changes things for the better. Still, all change demands a price, and the cured man had to pay his.

First Reactions

Upon his return, "his neighbors and the people who had been accustomed to see him begging began to ask, 'Isn't this the fellow who used to sit and beg?' Some were claiming it was he; others maintained it was not but someone who looked like him" (9:8-9, an echo of the divided opinions about Jesus reported in 8:40-43). One wouldn't think the ability to see would confuse people so much. The man had not changed externally. Why should he be so hard to recognize? Two reasons are possible.

First, many of the people probably assumed that no change in the man's condition was possible. Therefore what they observed demanded a different explanation. Their preconceptions, their reliance on external authority, their judgment by appearances overruled their own eyes.

Second, these same people probably never paid very close attention to the man when he was blind. They were accustomed to seeing him in a sitting posture, not standing; they heard his voice but didn't look at his face; they walked past him but he didn't approach them. In short, they didn't really know him before he received his sight. Both points apply to theological reflection.

Those who reflect theologically do not come to the task empty-headed. They have previous learning, personal convictions, prescribed messages which they are ready to apply to any situation. They may expect reality as it occurs to fit their understanding as it has developed, and most of the time people do see what they are looking for. Consequently, they don't pay close attention to everyday events. Theological reflection tries to get them to pay closer attention to the testimony of experience.

"The man himself said, 'I am the one' " (9:9). In John's Gospel "I am" statements are always revelatory. This one is not in the same class with Jesus' self-declarations, of course, but God's works are showing forth in this man all the same, just as Jesus desired in verse three. The people reacted to him as they frequently reacted to Jesus: they wanted an explanation.

" 'How were your eyes opened?' " (9:10). They assumed

and demanded an empirical explanation. This is not a bad start. Theological reflection adheres to events as they occur and trusts that the most factual account will lead to the most telling insight. That's why the basis for theological reflection is usually a specific case, a critical incident, or a verbatim dialogue.

"'That man they call Jesus made mud and smeared it on my eyes, telling me to go to Siloam and wash. When I did go and wash, I was able to see'" (9:11). An accurate account, at least according to John's report in verses six and seven. Clearly it pointed to Jesus as the central figure. So the people asked the next logical question.

"'Where is he?'" This is the quest of theological reflection: to locate the divine presence in the facts that have been assembled. But the man replied with complete candor, "'I have no idea'" (9:12). In most situations the divine presence is not self-evident and the observations of an outsider can help — a prime benefit of group discussion. The crowd seemed to know this.

Experts

"Next, they took the man who had been born blind to the Pharisees" (9:13). Why go to the Pharisees? John explains by inserting a fact not mentioned earlier (just as students may omit important details in their initial description). "Note that it was on a sabbath that Jesus had made the mud paste and opened his eyes" (9:14). The fact of the sabbath suggested which experts to consult. Theological reflection uses the same criterion. It lets the facts of an experience suggest the theological sources to consult.

This phase of the story opens rather ominously. The image of the man being taken to the Pharisees anticipates

Jesus being taken from one authority to another during his trial. Moreover, the man was brought to the Pharisees because of a sabbath violation, not the healing of his blindness, even though the Pharisees began with the latter point (9:15).

The man recounted his story, but it was obvious that the Pharisees had their own agenda. Although the healed man did not mention the sabbath in his account of the cure, the Pharisees responded with a familiar accusation, "'This man [Jesus] cannot be from God because he does not keep the sabbath'" (9:16). Some of the "others" tried to bring the discussion back to the main point. "'If a man is a sinner, how can he perform signs like these?'" (9:16). The Pharisees had not accused him of being a sinner, although the inference was clear from their statement of principle in verse sixteen. The discussion was jumping around and not going anywhere. "They were sharply divided over him" (9:16).

Theological reflection in a group faces the same possibility. Individuals may have their own agenda and firm convictions about certain points. Discussion can go in many directions and generate strong feelings. In itself this is the character of theological reflection. It is a search, probing for the hidden element that will reveal meaning, not a carefully reasoned lecture. It is undertaken by people who have stake in the issues; it is not a cerebral inquiry for its own sake. When group reflection works well, it finds its way back to the experiential starting point.

Personal Testimony

"Then they addressed the blind man again: 'Since it was your eyes he opened, what do you have to say about him?'" (9:17). In a theological reflection group everybody is a participant, but some preference is given to those whose experience is being reflected upon. It isn't that they automatically know what their experience means theologically. If they did, theological reflection would be unnecessary. Rather, priority is given because the experience is theirs. They are on the inside of it; they have the best sense of what is congruent with it and what isn't. Others can enter the experience, but no one else can live it as their own.

The man made the most of his privileged position. "'He is a prophet'" (9:17). In light of the accusation the Pharisees had already delivered, this was a bold assertion, perhaps stemming from the man's impatience. It was as if he was in a hurry to see all he had missed, to describe all that entered his vision while it was still day. He wanted nothing more to do with darkness or this discussion. His dialogue partners were not quite that eager. They had more angles to investigate.

". . . [T]hey summoned the parents of this man who now could see. 'Is this your son and if so, do you attest that he was blind at birth? How do you account for the fact that now he can see?'" (9:18-19). The parents knew only what they knew: this is our son; he was born blind. How he was cured or who did it, we have no idea (9:20-21). (The fact that both the man born blind and his parents "have no idea" who or where Jesus is recalls that theological reflection does not always have clear concepts and precise knowledge about the divine presence in the experience it investigates.)

The parents withdrew from the discussion and put the focus back on their son. "'Ask him. He is old enough to speak for himself'" (9:21). John makes clear the motive for their suggestion. "His parents answered in this fashion because they were afraid of the Jews, who had already agreed among themselves that anyone who acknowledged Jesus as the Messiah would be put out of the synagogue" (9:22). The man had not acknowledged Jesus as the Messiah, but calling him a prophet was getting too close for comfort. His parents, who had already been victimized by their son's blindness (was it their sin that had caused this?), didn't want to be punished for his ability to see too.

There are many reasons why people may hesitate to share their own views in theological reflection. Most of them involve self-protection. What will they think of me if I say this? Will I be labeled? Will my effectiveness be hurt? Will they think I'm a faithful Christian, a good minister, a loyal member of the church? While these are fair questions, they have a tendency to paralyze theological reflection because they close off avenues of inquiry and settle for safe theological opinions.

"A second time they summoned the man who had been born blind and said to him, 'Give glory to God! First of all we know this man is a sinner'" (9:24). The seeing man was getting impatient. Everything had become new to him. The descriptions he had heard in the darkness didn't begin to convey what he now could see for himself. Once again he responded out of his own experience. "'I do not know whether he is a sinner or not,' he answered. 'I know this much: I was blind before; now I can see'" (9:25). The Pharisees weren't satisfied. They wanted to go over the same story one more time.

Confrontation

"'Why do you want to hear it all over again? Do not tell me you want to become his disciples too?'" (9:27, an ironic paraphrase of the question the Pharisees put to the temple guard in 7:45-52). Aside from the sarcasm of this comment (and the role reversal which John's Gospel is fond of), a keen insight into theological reflection can be gleaned here. The purpose of reflection is to become disciples, to learn from actual experience what it means to follow Jesus. Sometimes this happens in spite of ourselves. People may enter a reflection confident they know what their theology means. As they pay attention to the experience, enter its inner contours, apply their previous knowledge, and listen to others, they begin to alter their previous theology, or at least to question it, before they are aware of doing so. When they do become aware, they must either pursue the change or cut it off. The Pharisees cut it off.

" 'You are the one who is that man's disciple. We are disciples of Moses. We know that God spoke to Moses, but we have no idea [once again] where this man comes from' " (9:28-29). They were unable to let this new experience mingle with a tradition made solemn by God's discourse with Moses. In this regard the Pharisees raise a valuable caution for theological reflection. It should not be subversive or reckless, eager to toss aside anything which doesn't immediately fit with present experience. Rather the new must be measured by the established, especially if the new is as startling as being able to see for the first time. It is this measurement that theological reflection seeks: the interplay and integration of present experience with tradition.

The seeing man attempted this, albeit with a snide opening. " 'Well, this is news! You do not know where he comes from, yet he opened my eyes' " (9:30). Here are the two central elements — an indisputable fact and an ambiguous meaning. The fact is that the man can see, but what this means in the established interpretive scheme is not clear. The man had his own explanation.

" 'We know that God does not hear sinners, but that if someone is devout and obeys his will, he listens to him.

It is unheard of that anyone ever gave sight to a person blind from birth. If this man were not from God, he could never have done such a thing'" (9:31-33).

When you start with experience, the logic is irrefutable. A good deed has been done. A good person must have done it (God does not hear sinners). Jesus did it, therefore he must be a good person (if not a prophet or the Messiah). Yet the same logic doesn't work the other way around. A good person obeys the law of Moses. The law forbids work on the sabbath. This man worked on the sabbath, therefore he is not good.

The conflict of these logics occupies much of the Gospel and should not be oversimplified. Nor should the Pharisees be caricatured as rigidly holding out for abstract principles in the face of contradictory evidence (even if the New Testament seems to portray them that way). But this conflict does epitomize one of the challenges of theological reflection in a group. What one person sees from the vantage point of personal experience is not always visible from the vantage point of others' formal knowledge. If one person affirms what an experience reveals, others may declare that this view isn't tenable (because they don't know where it comes from) and should not be held lest it lead a person outside the home of orthodoxy.

"'What,' they exclaimed. 'You are steeped in sin from your birth and you are giving us lectures?' With that they threw him out bodily" (9:34). Such a price is rarely paid for doing theological reflection (at least in the United States), although no doubt instances of expulsion from seminary, elimination from a congregation, or excommunication from a church have occurred because of contrary views. Nevertheless, it is more likely that theological reflection might create some unexpected discomfort or leave some unresolved questions. Hopefully it also leads to a new encounter with the Lord.

Recognition

"When Jesus heard of his expulsion, he sought him out and asked him, 'Do you believe in the Son of Man?'" (9:35). The consolation of this passage is that Jesus took the initiative (as he had with the disciples on the sea in chapters six and twenty-one). He sought out the man precisely when he had been abandoned by everyone else. Theological reflection in a group tries to prevent such abandonment by supporting a person's search for the divine presence even though the group may have "no idea" when or where it will come from this time. A reflection group can also make it easier to ask the honest question of the seeing man, "'Who is he, that I may believe in him?'" (9:37) and to hear the answer coming from experience, "'You have seen him. He is speaking to you now'" (9:38). At such a moment only an affirmation of faith is appropriate. "'I do believe, Lord,' he said, and bowed down to worship him" (9:38).

But Jesus wasn't finished. "'I came into this world to divide it, to make the sightless see and the seeing blind'" (9:39). Like many other paradoxical sayings of Jesus, this one reflects his own (or his disciples') perception of what really happened in his ministry rather than what he set out to do. In the same way, theological reflection sets out to enhance people's vision and to help them see God's works in their lives, but it can be divisive when it confronts their previous understanding and challenges their customary pattern of doing things.

"'You're not calling us blind, are you?'" the Pharisees asked him (9:40). A reflection group may wonder, "You're not saying we should scrap our theology, are you? You're not saying we don't know our own experience, are you?" Jesus clarified his position, and that of theological reflection.

" 'If you were blind, there would be no sin in that. "But we see," you say, and your sin remains' " (9:41). Not to see and to admit it opens the way for the light of the world (through theological reflection). Even those blind from birth can be given sight. But not to see and deny it hastens nightfall and perpetuates the darkness. The stakes in theological reflection are not as ultimate as Jesus' confrontation with sin in this passage, but his statements do underscore a necessary attitude for theological reflection.

To do theological reflection is to begin a search, often in darkness, with the confidence that light is to be found. Some of the procedures may seem as unfamiliar as smearing mud and spit on your eyes; some of the discussion may confuse friends and experts who don't hear the explanations they expect and begin to wonder what's happening to you. At some point experience beckons authority and tradition to speak their word, but the result can be unpredictable. Eventually you have to claim what experience reveals to you — and wait. Wait for the reappearance of the one who started all this, who wants to make the sightless see, who wants you to keep using your eyes and declaring what they show you.

SUMMARY

From this episode come the following lessons about theological reflection in a group.

1. A group can keep individuals from rushing to a

theological interpretation or settling for the first thought that comes to mind.

2. A group can insure that all relevant points of view are included, especially of those who were part of the original event but are not part of the reflection group.

3. A group sometimes operates with an unexpressed consensus about what is acceptable theologically and imposes this on new ideas.

4. A group helps to uncover pertinent facts some of which an individual may overlook.

5. A group can sense when outside experts are needed and can often recommend appropriate experts.

6. A group asks for a story to be retold, thereby clarifying what might have been missed or misinterpreted originally.

7. A group can balance one line of thought by providing alternative explanations.

8. Everyone in a reflection group should participate, but the presenter has a privileged position because originally the experience was his or hers.

9. Some members may withdraw from a group discussion to protect themselves if they feel the group is too threatening.

10. A group can sometimes confront an individual with the need for changes more convincingly than another individual can.

11. A group keeps individual experiences from assuming too much importance.

CHAPTER 6

From Reflection to Praxis

When the fruit of theological reflection on one event is used to shape the events which follow, it is rightly called praxis. Praxis is the action that flows from and gives expression to the insights of theological reflection.

The biggest challenge is to let the praxis emerge from the reflection rather than predetermining a course of action and then looking for theological reasons to justify it. The latter is not necessarily erroneous, but it is not the praxis which theological reflection promotes.

The eventual praxis is not known when a group begins to reflect theologically. They may know that they have to make a certain decision or respond to a particular crisis, but the exact decision or response is not yet determined. Sometimes a group has to restrain its desire to act in order to let the reflection mature and run its course; at other times a group has to refrain from endlessly discussing an issue in order to take action. In either case the praxis should be a demonstrable, behavioral embodiment of the reflection itself. Ideally one should be able to reconstruct the gist of the reflection from the praxis which results; at least, the reflection and the praxis should be consistent and clarify each other.

It is not easy to make the transition from reflection to praxis. In at least one instance — when his friend Lazarus died — it wasn't easy for Jesus either. When read from the point of view of theological reflection praxis, this episode offers some valuable insights.

THE RAISING OF LAZARUS

Prelude

The story begins with basic information, much as a case study or verbatim might. "There was a certain man named Lazarus who was sick. He was from Bethany, the village of Mary and her sister Martha" (11:1). Although Lazarus is introduced first, the sisters, especially Mary, are the pivotal characters. The village is identified through them; Mary is mentioned, parenthetically, as the one who will anoint Jesus in the next chapter; and it is the sisters who "sent word to Jesus to inform him, 'Lord, the one you love is sick'" (11:3).

This opening scene is filled with feeling. Lazarus's illness was obviously serious and cause for worry; Jesus' love for Lazarus, extended to the sisters (11:5), intensified the emotion. How did Jesus respond? "After hearing that Lazarus was sick, he stayed on where he was for two days more" (11:6). An experienced pastoral minister might sense that Jesus was denying the impending threat of death and avoiding its painful implications. John offers a different explanation.

"This sickness is not to end in death; rather it is for God's glory, that through it the Son of God may be glorified" (11:4). If a student in a theological reflection group offered this thought, the group would likely criticize it as wishful thinking or a theological cop-out. It doesn't seem to address the issue directly, substituting a pious sentiment for the messy prospect of finding God in the midst of Lazarus's suffering. But for Jesus it is a conviction that calls for praxis.

"Let us go back to Judea" (11:7). If the Son of God is to be glorified through Lazarus's illness, then Jesus should be where Lazarus is. The praxis flows from the conviction. There was only one problem. Jesus and his disciples had just left that area because his opponents had "tried to arrest him" (10:39). Going back was a praxis that didn't make much sense to the disciples. Besides, they were dealing with their own emotion — fear of the authorities — and immediately tried to justify their preference for staying put. "Rabbi, with the Jews only recently trying to stone you, you are going back up there again?" (11:8).

Whoever ventured this suggestion must have wanted to retract it at once, for Jesus jumped on it with a cryptic reference to walking in the light rather than the darkness. This is a recurring theme in John's Gospel and in view of what will happen in Bethany it has a predictive quality, but it certainly did not ease the anxiety which originally prompted the disciples' question. Nor did Jesus clarify matters with his assurance, "Our beloved Lazarus has fallen asleep and I am going there to wake him" (11:11).

The danger of his proposed praxis seemed even less warranted in this case, and the disciples drew the obvious implication. "Lord, if he is asleep his life will be saved" (11:12), in contrast to their lives, which would be in jeopardy if they went to Bethany. Just as "the Jews" misunderstood Jesus' reference to rebuilding the temple (2:21-22), so the disciples misunderstood his reference to Lazarus's sleep. Their dullness compelled Jesus to speak the awful, unavoidable words, "Lazarus is dead" (11:14).

If Jesus did not want to face the fact that Lazarus was near death when he first received the news, the disciples' innocent questioning now forced him to face reality. But for Jesus reality was always more than it seemed to everyone else and it called for a praxis that was hard to understand. "For your sakes I am glad I was not there that you may come to believe" (11:15). This statement sounds like a desperate attempt to find meaning in a hopeless situation and maybe repress Jesus' own pain for the sake of consoling his disciples. Whatever it was, it did not deter his praxis. "In any event let us go to him."

Thomas, who did not accept the word of others easily, gave in. "Let us go along, to die with him" (11:16). This was compliance, not praxis. Thomas didn't want to die, and he probably didn't understand why Jesus wanted to take such a risk. Perhaps he was being sarcastic; perhaps he trusted that Jesus knew how to avoid his enemies; perhaps he just wanted to see what would happen; in the end he deferred to the only authority who could get him to act in ignorance.

The praxis of going to Lazarus was prompted not by the news of his illness but by reflection on its meaning. Jesus saw it as an occasion for God's glory, as an example of walking in the light, as an opportunity to strengthen the belief of his disciples. These are just the kinds of conclusions which theological reflection might reach, but they could not be enacted by remaining absent, by hiding, by keeping belief immune from testing. At the same time the praxis which the situation called for was disruptive and dangerous, and not everyone agreed with it. Sometimes it is harder to achieve consensus about praxis than it is about analysis or interpretation, especially when the praxis is uncomfortable or threatening. Even when consensus is achieved, the praxis still has to be carried out, and that can entail some unexpected surprises.

Theological Reflection

By the time Jesus and his disciples arrived, Lazarus had been dead for four days and the mourning rites were underway. Martha heard that Jesus was coming and went out to meet him before he even got to the village (11:20). This fits the reputation tradition has given her as being hyperactive, alert to every detail and anticipating tasks that need doing. Mary, on the other hand, "sat at home," the exact position she occupied in Luke's account (10:39).

Martha's opening comment to Jesus may be read in a pious fashion, expressing complete confidence in him and acceptance of whatever he decides. "Lord, if you had been here, my brother would never have died. Even now, I am sure that God will give you whatever you ask of him" (11:21-22). This reading softens her feelings and subordinates them to belief in whatever will follow — exactly the sentiment intended by the Gospel as it builds toward its own theological climax.

If the same passage were read from a clinical perspective, as one might read a student's verbatim, it has a different sound. Martha is grieving for her dead brother. Jesus has just showed up, a week after receiving her urgent message. The woman who on another occasion didn't hesitate to interrupt Jesus and tell him to send Mary into the kitchen might very well have confronted Jesus now with her understandable (even justified) anger. "Lord, where have you been? Didn't you get my message? Lazarus wanted to see you so badly. Why didn't you come? And what are you going to do about it now?"

Read either way Jesus responded as many ministers might when confronted with an uncomfortable, even embarrassing, situation. He theologized. "Your brother will rise again" (11:23). Martha concurred. "I know he will rise again in the resurrection on the last day" (11:24). This was not to be taken for granted. Many Jews at the time did not believe in any kind of resurrection. Jesus may have discussed this very point with Lazarus *and* his sisters on other visits. If so, he was recalling it now as a consolation for Martha, and perhaps for himself as well. At least he connected this belief with himself and hinted at its implications for praxis.

"I am the resurrection and the life; whoever believes in me, though he should die, will come to life; and whoever is alive and believes in me will never die" (11:26). These are action words; they move from general belief in the resurrection to specific belief in Jesus, and they concretize that belief in terms of Lazarus, who is dead, and Martha, who is alive. They call for the corresponding action of a decision. "Do you believe this?"

"Yes, Lord. I have come to believe that you are the Messiah, the Son of God: he who is to come into the world" (11:27). This explicit admission of faith goes beyond the implicit confession of the Samaritan woman at the well (4:29) or Peter after the feeding of the multitude (6:69). It is the moment of faith around which the Gospel pivots, and it is the culmination of theological reflection. But Lazarus was still in the tomb.

Praxis

Martha returned to the house and whispered to Mary, "The Teacher is here, asking for you" (11:28). Only Jesus could make Mary move so quickly. She left the house abruptly, and the mourners thought she was going to the tomb, so they went along to console her (11:29-31). But Mary headed straight for Jesus. When she saw him, she fell at his feet (where she sat in Luke's Gospel and where she would be while anointing Jesus in the next chapter of John's Gospel). Mary may not have been as assertive as Martha, but her opening remark, exactly the same as Martha's, evoked a deep emotional reaction from Jesus.

Instead of consoling Mary with theological reflection as he had Martha, Jesus was "troubled in spirit, moved by the deepest emotions" (11:33). Perhaps it was the sight of Mary weeping and the mourners echoing her grief, perhaps it was the inability to keep his own grief in check any longer that moved Jesus to action. "Where have you laid him?" (11:34).

Jesus' arrival was an incomplete praxis until he actually beheld the tomb. The closer he approached, the more his emotional energy rose. "Jesus began to weep, which caused the Jews to remark, 'See how much he loved him!' " (11:36). Still, not everyone was impressed. "He opened the eyes of that blind man. Why could he not have done something to stop this man from dying?" (11:37) — the same sort of chiding Jesus will hear on the cross. There are always those who know of a better praxis — for someone else to carry out. Nonetheless, their challenge can intensify a person's feelings and suggest a praxis that had not been previously envisioned.

"Take away the stone." Once again Martha didn't hesitate to intervene. "Lord, it has been four days now; surely there will be a stench!" (11:39). Jesus turned her attention from pragmatic considerations to praxis. "Did I not assure you that if you believed, you would see the glory of God displayed?" (11:40). Actually, Jesus assured his disciples of this, not Martha. But at this point the focus is on praxis, not accuracy.

For Jesus, praxis meant embodying belief, acting consistently and boldly on the divine presence sensed in a situation. Sometimes this meant a physical healing, sometimes it meant spiritual counsel, sometimes it meant making a decision or taking a position. There was never a single praxis that fit all situations. The situation itself, and the divine presence which reflection recognized within it, shaped the praxis.

In this case it is not difficult to imagine that Jesus' fixation with God's glory as manifested in the raising of the dead, and his preoccupation with his own impending death rushed into the void created by Lazarus's death. These profound experiences swirled together and empowered Jesus to issue his summons, "Lazarus, come out!" (11:43).

This was not an attention-getting display or a privileged intervention reserved for a dear friend. It was the direct enactment of what Jesus believed and recognized in this situation. It was the conversion of reflection into praxis. But Jesus wasn't finished.

"Untie him and let him go free" (11:44). Praxis is rarely an extraordinary event, isolated from the flow of daily activities. It is the shaping of ordinary, daily events by reflection. Granted the resurrection of Lazarus was an extraordinary event, but Jesus' praxis was intended to insert the resuscitated Lazarus back into the course of everyday life, as John indicates in the next chapter by describing a banquet for Jesus which Lazarus attends (and Martha serves!).

Untying Lazarus and letting him go free is a poetic

description of the goal of theological reflection. It aims at loosening the mental and behavioral bonds that constrict people; it frees them to see and move in accord with the divine presence they recognize in their own experience. This does not mean erasing all norms or structure, but it can call for changes and sometimes these can be quite radical.

Praxis moves reflection from the level of insight to action, or, more accurately, the dynamic thrust of reflection itself moves from insight to action. Not just any action qualifies. Praxis is that action which results from careful and critical reflection on a situation. It is consistent with the full reality of the situation itself, and it always aims at giving glory to the God who is recognized in the situation.

Praxis is sometimes spontaneous. Jesus' raising of Lazarus can be read that way, as a decision and course of action which manifested itself to him only as he entered the situation, felt the grief of the sisters and his own pain, heard the challenge of the bystanders, confronted the stone tomb with his profound belief in God's power to raise the dead, and anticipated his own longing for that power to work through him.

At other times praxis is planned. It still comes as the result of theological reflection, but in this case a person structures a particular action to embody that reflection, to function as a symbolic deed which can elicit further reflection and praxis. On at least one occasion Jesus engaged in this type of praxis.

WASHING THE DISCIPLES' FEET

"Before the feast of Passover, Jesus realized that the hour had come for him to pass from this world to the Father"

(13:1). The setting is rich with liturgical meaning (as was Jesus' other planned praxis, the cleansing of the temple). Passover, the high cultic moment in the cycle of Jewish feasts, was soon to be celebrated. But Jesus would not just be celebrating it; he would be fulfilling it with his own passover. His hour, which controlled the action throughout the Gospel, had come; Judas was committed to handing him over; and Jesus was sharing a farewell meal with his disciples.

During the supper, Jesus rose, took off his cloak, and prepared to wash his disciples' feet (13:4-5). This was not a spontaneous gesture, much less a random impulse caused by Jesus' nervous anticipation of the next few days. It was an action that flowed directly from his reflection. "Fully aware that he had come from God and was going to God, the Father who had handed everything over to him," Jesus began his symbolic action. This praxis embodied his understanding.

Peter balked. "Lord, are you going to wash my feet?" (13:6). This action was clearly out of character, and Peter knew it. He must have felt uncomfortable being served by his master and could not hide his reaction. Most reflection leaders would welcome participants like Peter who don't have to be coaxed or tricked into expressing their feelings. Jesus was equally receptive. "You may not realize now what I am doing, but later you will understand" (13:7). He knew that this deed was not self-evident; he expected the disciples to ponder it, to uncover its meaning gradually.

Peter was a man of the moment, compulsive and demanding. "You will never wash my feet." Jesus was just as adamant. "If I do not wash you, you will have no share in my heritage" (13:8). For Christian theology this passage has a clear reference — the importance of baptism; for theological reflection it also has a clear message. The meaning of planned praxis cannot be discerned from the outside. A person has to enter in and be affected by the action in order to grasp its meaning.

Peter got the point. With typical exuberance he announced, "Lord, then not only my feet, but my hands and head as well" (13:9). If washing was the thing, then wash everything. Peter wanted to be totally involved, to experience everything — though not necessarily to reflect on it. Jesus drew him back to the symbolic nature of the action and the reflective purpose of it. "The man who has bathed has no need to wash" (13:10). Jesus was not washing the disciples hygienically; he was bathing them symbolically in order to communicate a point.

"Do you understand what I just did for you?" (13:12). He did not wait for an answer, especially not from Peter. This was a rhetorical question intended to peak their interest in the answer he would give. "You address me as 'Teacher' and 'Lord,' and fittingly enough, for that is what I am." So far so good. The disciples could nod in assent to this unquestioned fact.

"But . . ." Inevitably there is a "but." Praxis does not always leave familiar and established knowledge intact. It has its own lessons and its own implications. "If I washed your feet — I who am Teacher and Lord — then you must wash each other's feet." One can almost see the disciples glancing at each other, wondering who would wash the smelly feet of the fishermen or how Thomas or Nathanael would ever wash anyone's feet.

Jesus clarified. "What I just did was to give you an example: as I have done, so you must do" (13:15). His praxis was not about washing feet; it was about relating to one another. He used an outrageous example to redefine the way he expected them to interact when he was no longer with them. He demonstrated the behavior; he implicated them in it; and he invited them to reflect on it. "Once you know all these things, blest will you be if you put them into practice" (13:17).

Praxis has the same power today. A well-thought-out, symbolic action can summon people's attention and help them come to the insight which originally inspired the action. In this case (as with the foot washing), praxis can have a pedagogical value. In theological reflection groups this happens most often in role plays. If the situation has been carefully designed and the roles clearly defined, participants can acquire theological insights that they would not have learned in the classroom and may not have encountered in their own experience.

Ideally praxis is either the deliberate enactment of careful reflection or a planned action illustrating a specific theological point. Realistically, however, a minister is often in a situation which calls for an immediate response with no time for extensive theological reflection. In this case praxis embodies the general reflection a minister has done previously. Jesus once found himself in such a situation, and his response is again instructive for the praxis of theological reflection.

CANA

John begins this episode with the striking notice, "On the third day . . ." (2:1). A Christian reader is immediately alerted that something remarkable is going to happen even though the situation is very familiar — a wedding celebration. For John this was the third day in the unfolding drama that began with the testimony of John the Baptizer and continued with Jesus' calling of the disciples. For Jesus this was a time to celebrate with his family, friends, and new disciples. The prospects for theological reflection or startling praxis seemed minimal in this setting, as they often do in the routine events of life or ministry.

Then a crisis occurred; the wine ran out. Mary became aware of it, perhaps because she was the hostess, perhaps because she was observant. In any event she brought the problem to Jesus. "They have no more wine" (2:3). It is not clear what she expected Jesus to do, but it is clear that he wanted to do nothing. "Woman, how does this concern of yours involve me?" Lest this seem too curt, John adds the reason: "My hour has not yet come" (2:4).

Most ministers can identify with Jesus' reaction. They go to a party to have a good time, to take a break from the responsibilities of being a pastor. Then a problem arises or a question is asked and they're expected to deal with it. It doesn't matter that this isn't a suitable occasion or a convenient time. The matter cannot be put off. Neither could Mary.

"Do whatever he tells you," she instructed those waiting on table. If Jesus had already planned the praxis that would open his public ministry, the cleansing of the temple (narrated by John in the second half of this chapter), then he must have felt acutely pressured by this situation. There was more at stake than the bad timing of his mother's request. If he intervened here, it could distract attention from his planned intervention at the temple. His mission was not to save face for obscure newlyweds but to restore the glory of God. How could he do both?

Jesus' praxis became a model for many of his subsequent signs. He took what was available — in this case, the stone water jars used for ceremonial washings — gave instructions about what to do with them, then disappeared before the effects were fully known. He repeated this pattern with the royal official (4:46-54), the sick man at Bethesda (5:1-15), the multitude whom he fed (6:1-15), and the man born blind (9:1-41). In each case people were left to interpret the action for themselves.

At Cana the waiter in charge remarked to the groom, "People usually serve the choice wine first; then, when the guests have been drinking awhile, a lesser vintage. What you have done is keep the choice wine until now" (2:10). The waiter in charge must have felt very clever for figuring this out; the groom must have been dumbfounded; and Mary must have been pleased.

Some situations, like the crisis at this wedding party, are almost defined by the need to do something. Under such pressure, it may seem that theological reflection has no place. Indeed, Jesus may have preferred to discuss the importance of "his hour" with his mother or to consult with his disciples so they wouldn't misinterpret his premature action or even to use the changed water as a point of departure for a theological lesson — as he would with the Samaritan woman in chapter four.

The situation, however, did not allow time for a new reflection. It demanded an immediate praxis that had to flow from Jesus' previous meditation, thereby expressing the convictions which had been accumulating in his mind. Reflection was still converted into praxis, a praxis which may have contained theological lessons not seen clearly in previous reflections.

SUMMARY

The chief lessons about converting reflection to praxis are these.

1. Praxis should emerge from the reflection itself and embody its insights, in contrast to action which is undertaken and then justified or explained theologically.

2. Praxis sometimes involves uncomfortable or even risky actions.

3. Compliance or habitual action is not praxis; praxis is the result of a deliberate reflection and choice.

4. The typical praxis of many ministers when confronted with other people's strong feelings is to theologize rather than to enter in and share the feelings.

5. Once praxis begins, it can evolve and change in unexpected ways due to the circumstances and ongoing impact of the experience.

6. Praxis is an expression of oneself and one's beliefs; it is not impersonal activity.

7. Praxis can be planned as a symbolic action intended to convey a message.

8. Planned praxis can often be imitated or adapted to new circumstances.

9. A role play is one type of planned praxis that can be very helpful in acquiring new skills or testing oneself in new circumstances.

CHAPTER 7

The Action-Reflection Cycle

Theological reflection usually concentrates on specific, discrete events. While this approach helps reflectors to discover the richness of each experience, it can also obscure the fact that every event is part of a continuous series and does not really exist in isolation from everything which precedes it and results from it.

To be consistent with this holistic view of reality, theological reflection should be a continuous, habitual activity. In addition, theological reflection is a skill, and like any skill it needs to be used continually for maximum benefit.

An individual or a group may begin with a single episode and methodically reflect on its theological meaning. When the outcome of this reflection is put into practice (praxis), it becomes a new experience which the individual or group can again reflect upon. This reflection gives rise to another praxis which calls for new reflection. In this way a cycle of theological reflection is gradually built up. The steps of a method become less rigid and the ability to recognize the divine presence in daily activities becomes more facile.

The starting point, however, remains the specific occurrence which stimulates reflection.

Most of the events in John's Gospel, as in the synoptics, are presented without much connection to other events. This is largely due to the nature of the Gospels, which are proclamations of faith rather than chronicles of events. Because they are presented as discrete episodes, these accounts can reinforce the idea that each occurrence is self-contained as is the theological reflection upon it.

There is one incident in John which dispels this impression and gives a glimpse of the continuous sequence which theological reflection encourages. It fills the whole of chapter six.

FEEDING OF THE MULTITUDE

In chapter five Jesus healed the man by the Sheep Pool and then got into a dispute with "the Jews," who confronted him for performing this work on the sabbath and making himself equal to God. "Later on," begins chapter six, as if intentionally connecting it with chapter five, "Jesus crossed the Sea of Galilee to the shore of Tiberias" (6:1). The connection continues with the observation, "a vast crowd kept following him because they saw the signs he was performing for the sick" (6:2), such as the cure in chapter five.

Jesus' prior action, the healing, led to a theological reflection with "the Jews" which ended with Jesus parting company from his opponents. His action of departing immediately created the setting for a new reflection, which John introduces by saying, "Jesus then went up the mountain and sat down there with his disciples" (6:3).

Although the crowds were not as disturbed as the authorities that Jesus performed his works on the sabbath, that didn't mean they had grasped the deeper meaning he intended to convey. By going up the mountain with his disciples, Jesus may have wanted to wean them away from a popular, superficial interpretation of his ministry and reflect with them more deeply on its implications. In any event, this is the type of continuous action-reflection cycle that enhances theological reflection.

By going up the mountain with his disciples, Jesus evokes the image of Moses, teacher par excellence. Indeed, this suggestion is confirmed by John's simple reference, "The Jewish feast of Passover was near" (6:4). Passover and Moses were inseparably linked. In addition, Passover implied food, eating the Passover meal, so "when Jesus looked up and caught sight of a vast crowd coming toward him (as the Israelites followed after Moses), he said to Philip, 'Where shall we buy bread for these people to eat?'" (6:5).

Even in the midst of the most important, private theological discussion, Jesus never forgot "the crowds" whose needs were to be served. Indeed, serving needs is the ultimate praxis of theological reflection.

Why ask Philip? Prior to this event, Philip was mentioned once before in John (2:43-46). When Jesus met him, he simply said, "Follow me." Obviously Philip did, but first he sought out Nathanael and said, "We have found the one Moses spoke of in the law." Philip's connection of Moses with Jesus may have prompted Jesus (or the Gospel author) to single him out in this situation, or it might have been Philip's appeal to action — "Come, see for yourself" — in responding to Nathanael's cynical comment, "Can anything good come from Nazareth?"

In either case Jesus was drawing on qualities he had

observed in Philip, qualities that made him seem appropriate to deal with the problem at hand — the same thing a good facilitator of a theological reflection group would do, inviting individuals who seem well suited to offer their opinions rather than calling on those who would almost surely fall short and feel unnecessary failure. But this time it didn't quite work.

Philip may have been spending too much time with Nathanael because he responded more as a pragmatic realist than an optimistic disciple. "Not even with two hundred days' wages could we buy loaves enough to give each of them a mouthful" (6:7). Nothing cuts off theological reflection more quickly than a problem-solving response, whether it is a critique of a proposed solution, as in Philip's comment, or an alternative solution, as in the response of Andrew.

"There is a lad here who has five barley loaves and a couple of dried fish. . . ." As soon as he said it, he must have realized the absurdity of his suggestion. "But what good is that for so many?" (6:9). Of course, the author of the Gospel is building dramatic intensity by contrasting the disciples' sense of futility with Jesus' eventual action. From a theological reflection point of view, the same contrast is instructive. Philip and Andrew were dealing with this situation at a needs-assessment level (just as theological reflectors can sometimes see only the emotional or psychological needs of a person). Jesus had a different angle.

Passover was near; he was breathing the air of this great feast; he saw the crowd and their hunger in theological terms. "Get the people to recline," he requested (6:10). Then he reenacted part of the Passover ritual, giving thanks for the available bread and fish, and passing them around. There is no explanation of how it happened (the Gospel is not on the level of Philip and Andrew, or merely curious readers), but everyone had enough to eat. In fact they had more than enough. The leftovers filled twelve baskets — an obvious reference to the new Israel emerging from the original Israel.

Jesus had answered his own question ("Where shall we buy bread for these people to eat?") by using a sound pastoral principle. *We* won't. Rather we'll search with the people for the resources they possess and use them, gratefully, to meet their needs. This was the same principle Jesus used with the man at the Sheep Pool in chapter five, with the Samaritan woman and royal official in chapter four, with Nicodemus in chapter three, and with the married couple at Cana in chapter two. Go within the situation, look for what is there, trust it, use it, enter through it into God's kingdom.

The crowd didn't quite catch his point. They had originally followed Jesus to this place because of the signs he was performing for the sick. This sign took them a step farther in their thinking, though not in the direction Jesus intended. "This is undoubtedly the Prophet who is to come into the world" (6:14). In Jesus they saw the Prophet who would take care of them, tell them what to believe, how to act. This Prophet, they believed, would take the place of the current crop of teachers and leaders.

Jesus sensed what was happening and "fled back to the mountain alone" (6:15). Perhaps he needed to reflect on what had developed (although in John's Gospel Jesus always knows ahead of time what he's going to do, as in 6:6). Perhaps he had to root the parallel with Moses more deeply in his own experience. Whatever the motive, the results of his reflection are shared in the rest of the chapter, interrupted by the appearance of Jesus to the disciples on the sea (previously discussed in chapter two).

The next day the crowd came back, but as Jesus was

nowhere to be found, the people started putting the facts together. There had been only one boat; the disciples had left without Jesus; the disciples had not come back, nor was Jesus in the vicinity. Therefore, they must all be in Capernaum. So off the crowd went to join them.

"When they found him on the other side of the lake, they said to him, 'Rabbi, when did you come here?' " (6:25). Instead of rejoicing that they had found him (and taking satisfaction in having figured out where he was), instead of learning from him why they had misinterpreted his act of feeding them, the crowd wanted to know when he had arrived — an indirect way of saying they were annoyed that he had left them waiting on the shore and had made them work so hard to catch up with him.

Sometimes those who do theological reflection are like this crowd. They show up to receive what is handed out. They settle for their first interpretation of events, and when they come back to an experience, they expect to find it exactly as it was when they left it. They think theological reflection is easier than it is, and they want its benefits without working too hard for them. Jesus' response challenges the motives of all theological reflectors.

"I assure you, you are not looking for me because you have seen signs but because you have eaten your fill of the loaves" (6:26). Like the Samaritan woman at the well, this crowd is not yet sufficiently interested in the spiritual significance of their experience; they remain on the level of obvious meaning and tangible satisfaction. For Jesus, as for theological reflection, this is just the beginning point, not the end point.

"You should not be working for perishable food but for food that remains unto life eternal, food which the Son of Man will give you; it is on him that God the Father has set his seal" (6:27). These are the themes which John has already introduced in Jesus' discussions with Nicodemus, the Samaritan woman, and the Jews who objected to his cure on the sabbath. But they are not merely repeated; each reflection opens the meaning wider, carries its implications farther, suggests action that flows from reflection.

The crowd seemed willing to accept Jesus' critique that they were working for perishable food, and asked, "What must we do to perform the works of God?" (6:28).

"Have faith in the One whom he sent." This is a nebulous work, not at all like rowing three or four miles in the dark against the wind as the disciples had done. In the same way it may seem easier to help solve people's problems than to do meaningful theological reflection. The crowd searched for a compromise, putting the task back on Jesus. "So that we can put faith in you, what sign are you going to perform for us to see? What is the 'work' you do?" (6:30).

Like "the Jews" who asked for a sign authorizing Jesus to cleanse the temple (2:18), the crowd wants a sign to assure them that their commitment will not be in vain. This is a puzzling demand since it was the signs Jesus performed for the sick which originally drew this crowd to him (6:2), and it was the sign of feeding them that prompted them to want to carry him off as their king (6:15) and to come looking for him the next day (6:24). The crowd seemed willing to go along but not to enter in; to analyze and comment on events but not to become part of what was happening; to adhere to their interpretation but not convert it to action — tendencies which appear in theological reflection as well.

To get the discussion started (and to further the Gospel's intent of portraying Jesus as the new Moses leading a new exodus), the crowd reasserted its interpretation of the previous day's sign, bolstering it with an appeal to tradition.

"Our ancestors had manna to eat in the desert; according to Scripture, 'He gave them bread from the heavens to eat'" (6:31). Their reference suggests that they do see Jesus as the new Moses ("the Prophet") feeding them. Are they correct? Isn't that having faith in him? Shouldn't that bring them their fill of loaves?

Jesus accepted the extent of their theological reflection but nudged it forward by making a point they could all affirm: behind Moses, behind every prophet, behind every good work is the one true God. "It was not Moses who gave you bread from the heavens; it is my Father who gives you the real heavenly bread" (6:32). Their response was predictable: "Sir, give us this bread always" (6:34). Jesus' response was revelatory: "I myself am the bread of life" (6:35).

Theological reflection aims at precisely this recognition: to see in the events of daily life the signs of God's presence and to interpret those signs accurately and fully so that the one who appears can say, "It is I," and the one who feeds can say, "I myself am the bread of life," and those who reflect can believe in him. This kind of recognition comes from the continuous interplay of event-reflection-praxis. The rewards are not always obvious at the outset, but they are real nonetheless.

"No one who comes to me shall ever be hungry, no one who believes in me shall ever thirst" (6:35). This was the same sentiment Jesus expressed to the Samaritan woman at the well, and it led her eventually to acknowledge him as the Messiah and to share her discovery with the villagers. Jesus seemed less confident of this crowd. "But as I told you — though you have seen me, you still do not believe" (6:36).

Jesus reflected on the bewildering testimony of human behavior. Everyone sees the same signs. For some, they are the keys to the kingdom; for others, they are the seeds of destruction. Who can figure? Only God knows why people respond the way they do. Jesus' role is to take those who believe in him, lose none of them, and raise them all up on the last day (6:37-40).

Of course, theological reflection leaders do not have that ultimate power or responsibility, nor do they have the capacity to insure that everyone will come to theological insight and deepen his or her faith as a result of reflecting together. What happens during a theological reflection period is as unpredictable and mysterious as what happened to the people who saw the signs Jesus performed. They liked the signs but not the interpretation. "At this the Jews [no longer just the crowd but now the antagonists from 2:18; 5:10, 18] started to murmur in protest because he claimed, 'I am the bread that came down from heaven'" (6:41). Jesus was leading them deeper into the mystery of the divine presence than they wanted to go. They defended their reluctance to move in his direction. "Is this not Jesus, the son of Joseph? Do we not know his father and mother? How can he claim to have come down from heaven?" (6:42). Nicodemus revisited.

From a theological reflection perspective they were not simply discrediting the messenger; they were finding it hard to believe that what was so familiar to them could be so revelatory, so ultimate, so divine. The immediate experiences which shape people's lives also carry this liability. It is hard to believe that they can be revelatory rather than repetitious, ultimate rather than ordinary, divine rather than distracting. It is nearly impossible to believe this if events are reflected upon only now and then, in isolation from the cumulative story they have to tell.

Jesus repeated his message. He could go no farther,

offer no more compelling evidence. It is the proof circle again: "Everyone who has heard the Father and learned from him comes to me" (6:45). If you have learned from God, you understand; you see what you have learned coming to life through me. If you haven't, you cannot come to me; you really don't see anything. This only increased the quarreling.

"How can he give us his flesh to eat?" They wouldn't move beyond their level of inquiry. Jesus wouldn't move from his level of meaning. No doubt this conversation occurred more than once (hint of a continuous reflection?), for John notes, "He said this in a synagogue instruction at Capernaum," implying perhaps that the repetition of Jesus' position in 6:53-59 took place at another time and in another setting, where "the Jews" were more prominent than just the crowds.

In fairness the questions raised by the crowd and "the Jews" were plausible enough, given their perspective on what Jesus was saying. They couldn't take the immediate leap that Philip and Andrew and Nathanael and Simon had taken when they first met Jesus. Even some of the disciples who frequently reflected with Jesus had trouble.

"This sort of talk is hard to endure! Who can take it seriously?" (6:60). Jesus, for one. He knew how serious the implications of his message were. "Jesus knew from the start, of course, the ones who refused to believe and the one who would hand him over" (6:64). With every reflection, the subsequent action intensified. "From this time on, many of his disciples broke away and would not remain in his company any longer" (6:66).

Jesus must have been hurt and disappointed, but he did not want to pressure anyone into staying with him, not even the Twelve. "Do you want to leave me too?" (6:67).

Theological reflection should never be coercive. It should rely on the intrinsic persuasion of the reflection rather than the control of a particular leader. Such freedom fosters faith. "Lord, to whom shall we go? You have the words of eternal life. We have come to believe; we are convinced that you are God's holy one" (6:68-69).

It was Peter speaking, for the first time in John's Gospel, and he spoke neither impetuously nor naively. He had been part of all these events, heard the words, seen the signs, listened to the debates. He went through the cycle of action-reflection often enough to come to this recognition, the climax of the Gospel and of theological reflection.

SUMMARY

Theological reflection is a skill which needs to be exercised continuously. Chapter six of John describes this process and teaches the following lessons.

1. Every event/action is potentially the basis for a new theological reflection, especially if the event/action results from a previous reflection.

2. Analyzing a situation in terms of needs to be met or problems to be solved is not very conducive to fostering a continuous action-reflection cycle.

3. Theological reflection can orient a person toward meanings and actions they would prefer to avoid, and it can require more effort than they are willing to make.

4. The action-reflection cycle demands that reflectors enter into the practical implications of their reflection and not remain intellectual bystanders.

5. The more continuous the reflection, the more chal-

lenging, and sometimes disturbing, the implications can be for action.

6. The action-reflection cycle should be persuasive, not coercive; people should not be pressured into a certain way of thinking or acting but should choose it in light of the reflection process.

Epilogue

This book ends where John's Gospel begins — with the prologue. The prologue is an intriguing instance of poetic, mystical, and cosmic references to God's Word, probably drawn from an early Christian hymn, interspersed with prosaic, historical references to the life of Jesus. The combination, woven together as it is, symbolizes the nature of theological reflection.

The prologue begins with the widest horizon of time and space: in the beginning, when all things came into being. The full sweep of reality is the stage for the Gospel to follow. Theological reflection operates within this same horizon. It is conscious of the pervasive presence of the Word, "apart from whom nothing came to be," and it seeks to discover that Word, to testify to the light which "shines on in the darkness."

Still, theological reflection testifies to the light not in cosmic, mystical terms but in the people, places, and events that make up human history. Accordingly, the transcendent vision of the opening verses is quickly brought to earth.

"There was a man named John, sent by God, who came as a witness to testify to the light."

John is the patron of theological reflection. His sole purpose was to testify to the light — not to be the light, only to point it out, to direct attention to it, to affirm that it was shining even in the midst of darkness. This is a difficult task. Nevertheless, the light of the Word is not so blinding that it is impossible to miss it or so otherworldly that it is impossible to avoid it.

But "the world did not know who he was . . . his own did not accept him." The creative harmony between the Word and the world exalted in the opening verses became confused, though not completely. There were some who recognized the Word and accepted him. Their reward was not measured in earthly terms, even though their recognition had occurred on earth. No, those who accepted the Word became children of God. This incredible transformation was not the product of human power, but the gift of divine power. And the same divine power that enabled humans to become children of God enabled the Word to become flesh. In the convergence of these two movements "the glory of an only Son coming from the Father, filled with enduring love" is manifest.

This is the vision that inspires theological reflection. It seeks to help people recognize the Word in the world and to accept him so they may become children of God. Those who do recognize it feel within themselves the same power which enabled the Word to become flesh, and thus share in the inner mystery of that event as well.

Like John, theological reflection hopes only to proclaim, "This is he of whom I said, 'The one who comes after me ranks ahead of me.'" The one who is revealed through reflection, after the descriptions and analyses and questions and insights, this is the one who was always, already there, before the process began.

The process leads through reflection to the fullness of life. "Of his fullness we have had a share — love following upon love." Reflection leads to recognition, recognition leads to attraction, attraction leads to union, union leads to action, and the whole process is wrapped in love. Theological reflection merely seeks to serve this process, to testify to its light, keeping in mind that "No one has ever seen God. It is God the only Son, ever at the Father's side, who revealed him" — and continues to reveal, through the engaging, challenging process served by theological reflection.